FEDERAL COORDINATOR

FOR

METEOROLOGICAL SERVICES AND SUPPORTING RESEARCH

8455 Colesville Road, Suite 1500
Silver Spring, Maryland 20910
301-427-2002
http://www.ofcm.noaa.gov/

NATIONAL HURRICANE OPERATIONS PLAN

http://www.ofcm.noaa.gov/nhop/13/nhop13.htm

FCM-P12-2014

Washington, D.C.
May 2014

CHANGE AND REVIEW LOG

Use this page to record changes and notices of reviews.

Change Number	Page Numbers	Date Posted (mm/dd/yyyy)	Initials
1.			
2.			
3.			
4.			
5.			

Changes are indicated by a vertical line in the margin next to the change or by shading and strikeouts.

No.	Review Date (mm/dd/yyyy)	Comments	Initials
1.			
2.			
3.			
4.			
5.			

FOREWORD

The Office of the Federal Coordinator for Meteorological Services and Supporting Research (OFCM) annually hosts the Interdepartmental Hurricane Conference (IHC) to provide a forum for the responsible Federal agencies, together with the user communities, such as emergency management, to review and improve the Nation's hurricane forecast and warning program.

The 2014 Tropical Cyclone Research Forum (TCRF)/68th IHC was conducted 3-6 March. The forum had a large "virtual" participation with two primary locations where attendees gathered to participate—the NOAA Center for Weather and Climate Prediction, College Park, MD, and the National Hurricane Center, Miami, FL. The OFCM-sponsored Working Group for Hurricane and Winter Storms Operations and Research (WG/HWSOR) met on the first day of the forum to review various action and informational items related to the hurricane program, including recommended changes to this plan, the *National Hurricane Operations Plan* (NHOP). The results of the meeting were presented by the WG/HWSOR chair during the forum's final plenary session. New procedures and agreements briefed at the forum were incorporated into this publication—the 52nd edition of the NHOP. This plan is published annually prior to the hurricane season and documents the interdepartmental effort to provide the United States and designated international recipients with forecasts, warnings, and assessments, concerning tropical and subtropical weather systems.

The WG/HWSOR addressed 20 action items. Of those, six were closed by incorporating changes into this edition of the NHOP, two items were deferred, and four items were for information only. The remaining items will be worked through follow-on actions by the group. Detailed descriptions of the action items are available on the OFCM's web site at http://www.ofcm.noaa.gov/homepage/text/spc_proj/ihc.html.

This edition of the NHOP includes a number of noteworthy changes including:

- Updated section 2.2.2, regarding the notification of JTWC on the issuance of Special Tropical Weather Outlooks by the NHC and CPHC.

- Updated section 5.5.1.1, regarding DoD weather reconnaissance support to NOAA.

- Revised tropical cyclone names and pronunciations (Tables 3-1 and 3-2).

- Updated Figure 5.10, depicting reconnaissance data links.

- Updated Vortex Data Message code in Chapter 5 with various format changes (Table 5-2, Figure 5-3, Item P).

- Updated flight altitudes and ensured consistency of pressure unit descriptors for tropical cyclone center fixes in section 5.4.1, Figures 5-3 and 5-4, and Table 5-2 .

- Added *Radar reflectivity imagery of the tropical cyclone inner's core* to paragraphs 5.4.1, 5.4.6, 5.7.1, and in the list of priorities in paragraph 5.4.1.

- Added contact information for the DoD Air Traffic Services Cell (ATSC) in Appendices M and N.

- Updated the aircraft transponder codes in paragraph 6.1.2.3.

The following summarizes the 2013 tropical cyclone season:

- For the Atlantic hurricane season, there were 13 named tropical storms, of which only two became hurricanes. Neither of these storms became a major hurricane for the first time since 1994.[1] This year's totals were below the 30-year (1981-2010) averages of 12 named storms, six hurricanes, and three major hurricanes.[2] Tropical cyclone activity in the Atlantic basin during 2013 was about 67 percent below the 1981-2010 median.[3]

- Hurricanes Ingrid and Manuel hit Mexico in 2013.[4] Hurricane Ingrid caused at least 32 deaths, and Manuel caused at least 123 deaths. Both names were retired by the World Meteorological Organization; Ingrid was replaced by "Imelda" and Manuel with "Mario" in the Eastern North Pacific name lists.[5]

- For the Eastern North Pacific (east of longitude 140W), there were 18 named storms (slightly above the long-term annual average).[6] Of these, eight became hurricanes (below the average of nine), and only one major hurricane (below the average of four); the accumulated cyclone energy was also below the long-term median.[7]

- For the Central Pacific, six tropical cyclones were identified—one tropical depression, four tropical storms, and one hurricane. This was slightly above the normal of four to five tropical cyclones for the basin.[8]

Both civilian and military organizations compromise the multiagency national tropical cyclone forecasting and warning system. As we strive to be a "Weather-Ready Nation," the efforts of these organizations, along with the reconnaissance aircrews, emergency managers, agency leaders, and others, help to prevent injuries and the loss of life, reduce vulnerability, and further improve weather services to the citizens of this Nation.

//SIGNED//

Samuel P. Williamson
Federal Coordinator for Meteorological
Services and Supporting Research

---

[1] http://www.nhc.noaa.gov/text/MIATWSAT.shtml
[2] 2013 NHC November Monthly Atlantic Tropical Weather Summary
[3] http://www.nhc.noaa.gov/text/MIATWSAT.shtml
[4] http://www.noaanews.noaa.gov/stories2014/20140410_hurricanenameretired.html
[5] IBID
[6] http://www.nhc.noaa.gov/text/MIATWSEP.shtml
[7] IBID
[8] http://www.ofcm.gov/ihc14/presentations/Session1/s01-01Evans.pdf

NATIONAL HURRICANE OPERATIONS PLAN

TABLE OF CONTENTS

LIST OF FIGURES

Figure

LIST OF TABLES

Table

CHAPTER 1

INTRODUCTION

1.1.   General. The tropical cyclone warning service is an interdepartmental effort to provide the United States and designated international recipients with forecasts, warnings, and assessments concerning tropical and subtropical weather systems. The National Oceanic and Atmospheric Administration (NOAA) of the Department of Commerce (DOC) is responsible for providing forecasts and warnings for the Atlantic and Eastern and Central Pacific Oceans while the Department of Defense (DOD) provides the same services for the Western Pacific and Indian Ocean (see Figure 1-1). NOAA, along with other Federal agencies such as the U.S. Navy and the National Aeronautics and Space Administration (NASA), also conducts supporting research efforts to improve tropical cyclone forecasting and warning services. The bottom line—this interdepartmental cooperation achieves economy and efficiency in the provision of the tropical cyclone forecasting and warning services to the Nation. The *National Hurricane Operations Plan* provides the basis for implementing agreements reached at the Interdepartmental Hurricane Conference (IHC), which is sponsored annually by the Office of the Federal Coordinator for Meteorological Services and Supporting Research. The goal of the IHC is to bring together the responsible Federal agencies to achieve agreement on items of mutual concern related to tropical cyclone forecasting and warning services for the Atlantic and Pacific Oceans.

1.2.   Scope. The procedures and agreements contained herein apply to the Atlantic Ocean, Gulf of Mexico, Caribbean Sea, and the Pacific Ocean. The plan defines the roles of individual agencies, participating in the tropical cyclone forecasting and warning program when more than one agency is involved in the delivery of service in any specific area. When a single agency is involved in any specific area, that agency's procedures should be contained in internal documents and, to the extent possible, be consistent with NHOP practices and procedures.

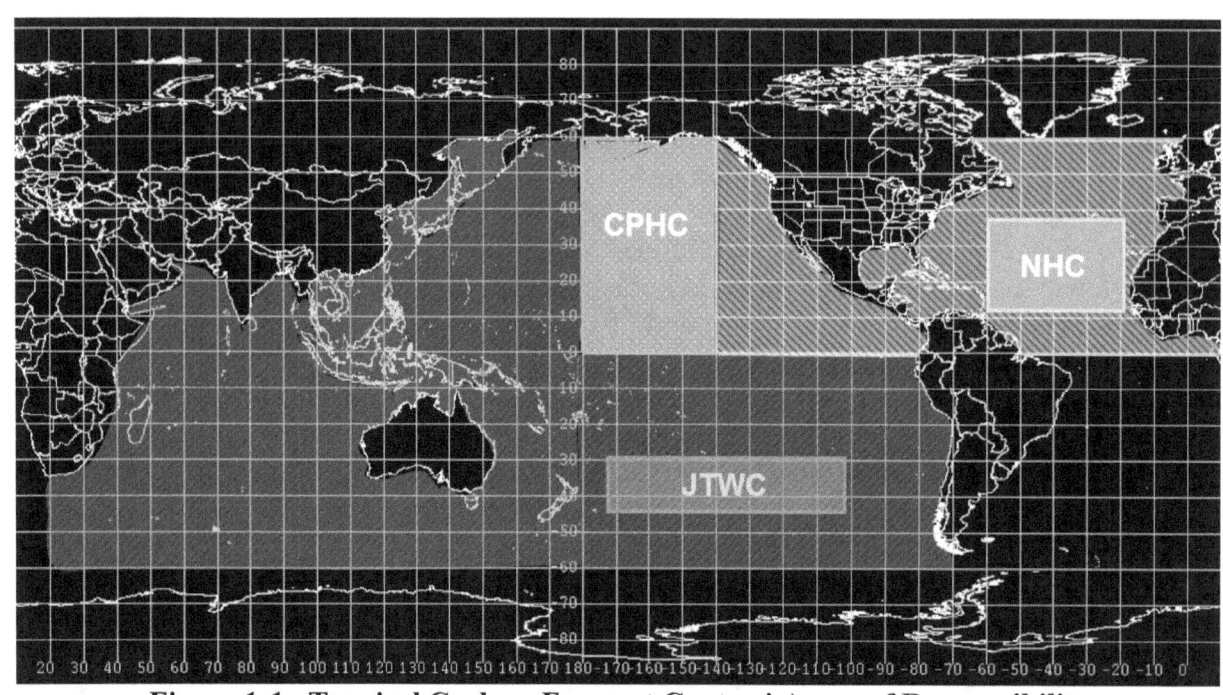

Figure 1-1. Tropical Cyclone Forecast Centers' Areas of Responsibility

CHAPTER 2

RESPONSIBILITIES OF COOPERATING FEDERAL AGENCIES

2.1. **General**. The Department of Commerce (DOC), through the National Oceanic and Atmospheric Administration (NOAA), is charged with the overall responsibility to implement a responsive, effective national tropical cyclone warning service. Many local, state, and Federal agencies play a vital role in this system; their cooperative efforts help ensure that necessary preparedness actions are taken to minimize loss of life and destruction of property. The joint participation by the Department of Defense (DOD), the Department of Transportation (DOT), and the Department of Homeland Security (DHS)/U.S. Coast Guard (USCG) with the DOC brings to bear those Federal resources considered essential for storm detection and accurate forecasting. This cooperative effort has proven to be a cost-effective, highly responsive endeavor to meet national requirements for tropical cyclone warning information.

2.2. **DOC Responsibilities**.

    2.2.1. **Forecasting and Warning Services.** The DOC will provide timely dissemination of forecasts, warnings, and all significant information regarding tropical and subtropical cyclones to the appropriate agencies, marine and aviation interests, and the general public.

    2.2.2. **Support to DOD.** Through NOAA's National Weather Service (NWS), the DOC will:

- Consult, as necessary, with the DOD regarding their day-to-day requirements for forecast/advisory services and attempt to meet these requirements within the capabilities of the tropical cyclone warning service.
- Provide, through the National Hurricane Center (NHC), the coordinated DOC requirements for weather reconnaissance and other meteorological data to be acquired by the DOD on tropical or subtropical cyclones and disturbances.
- Provide facilities, administrative support, and the means to disseminate meteorological data for the Chief, Aerial Reconnaissance Coordination, All Hurricanes (CARCAH) as agreed to by the DOC and DOD.
- Provide the DOD with basic meteorological information, warnings, forecasts, and associated prognostic reasoning concerning location, intensity, and forecast movement of tropical and subtropical cyclones in the following maritime areas, including the adjacent states and possessions of the United States:
  - Atlantic Ocean (north of the equator including the Caribbean Sea and Gulf of Mexico). Advisories are the responsibility of the Director, NHC, Miami, FL. The NHC will consult with the Fleet Weather Center, Norfolk, VA, prior to issuing initial and final advisories and prior to issuing any advisory that indicates a significant change in forecast of intensity or track from the previous advisory. Exchange of information is encouraged on subsequent warnings when significant changes are made or otherwise required.
  - Eastern Pacific Ocean (north of the equator and east of 140°W). Advisories are the responsibility of the Director, NHC, Miami, FL. The NHC will consult with

the Joint Typhoon Warning Center (JTWC), Pearl Harbor, HI, prior to issuing initial and final advisories and prior to issuing any advisory that indicates a significant change in forecast of intensity or track from the previous advisory. Exchange of information is encouraged on subsequent warnings when significant changes are made or otherwise required. The NHC will notify JTWC prior to issuance of a Special Tropical Weather Outlook (TWO).

- Central Pacific Ocean (north of the equator between 140°W and 180°). Advisories are the responsibility of the Director, Central Pacific Hurricane Center (CPHC), Honolulu, HI. In addition to the main Hawaiian Islands, CPHC also issues watches and warnings for Johnston Atoll, Midway, and the northwest Hawaiian Islands. The CPHC will consult with JTWC prior to issuing initial and final advisories and prior to issuing any advisory that indicates a significant change in forecast of intensity or track from the previous advisory. Exchange of information is encouraged on subsequent warnings when significant changes are made or otherwise required. The CPHC will notify JTWC prior to issuance of a Special Tropical Weather Outlook (TWO).
- West Pacific Ocean (Guam and Micronesia). Public advisories are prepared by the NWS Weather Forecast Office (WFO) Guam, using the tropical cyclone forecasts/advisories prepared by JTWC as guidance. WFO Guam issues watches and warnings for all tropical cyclones affecting the Territory of Guam, the Commonwealth of the Northern Marianas, the Republic of Palau, the Federated States of Micronesia, and the Republic of the Marshall Islands.

2.2.3. Post Analysis of Tropical Cyclones. The DOC, through NWS, will conduct an annual post analysis for all tropical cyclones in the Atlantic and the Pacific regions east of 180° and prepare an annual hurricane report for issue to interested agencies.

2.2.4. Environmental Satellite Systems. The National Environmental Satellite, Data, and Information Service (NESDIS) will:
- Operate DOC environmental satellite systems capable of providing coverage of meteorological conditions in the tropics during the tropical cyclone season, and monitor and interpret DOC satellite imagery.
- Obtain, as necessary, National Aeronautics and Space Administration (NASA) research and development satellite data and Defense Meteorological Satellite Program (DMSP) data for NWS operational use and to comply with NHC and CPHC satellite data requirements.
- Provide surveillance support with fixes and/or intensity estimates to the Joint Typhoon Warning Center (JTWC), NHC, and CPHC through analysis of all available satellite imagery.

2.2.5. Data Buoy Systems. Through the National Data Buoy Center (NDBC), the DOC will, subject to available funding, develop, deploy, and operate environmental data buoy systems and automated coastal stations to support the data requirements of NHC and CPHC.

2.2.6. Weather Reconnaissance. Through the NOAA Office of Marine and Aviation Operations (OMAO), DOC will provide weather reconnaissance flights, including synoptic surveillance, as specified in Chapter 5, unless relieved of these responsibilities by the Administrator of NOAA.

2.3. **DOD Responsibilities.** The DOD will:

- Disseminate significant meteorological information on tropical and subtropical cyclones to the NWS in a timely manner.
- Provide NHC and CPHC current DOD requirements for tropical and subtropical cyclone advisories.
- Meet DOC requirements for aircraft reconnaissance and other special observations as agreed to by DOD and DOC (see Appendix F).
- Provide at NHC a 24-hour aircraft operations interface—Chief, Aerial Reconnaissance Coordination, All Hurricanes (CARCAH).
- Designate CARCAH as the liaison to NHC. CARCAH will serve as NHC's point of contact to request special DOD observations in support of this plan (e.g., additional upper-air observations).
- Provide weather reconnaissance data monitor services to evaluate and disseminate reconnaissance reports.
- Provide surveillance support with fixes and/or intensity estimates to the Central Pacific Hurricane Center through analysis of available satellite imagery. The support is provided by the 17th Operational Weather Squadron Meteorological Satellite Operations (SATOPS) Flight (17 OWS/WXJ), Joint Typhoon Warning Center, Pearl Harbor, HI, and is focused on the Indian Ocean and the Central, South, and Northwest Pacific Ocean.
- Western Pacific Ocean (north of the equator): Provide NWS with basic meteorological information, forecasts, and associated prognostic reasoning, concerning location, intensity, wind distribution, and forecast movement of tropical cyclones for the Northwest Pacific west of 180°. JTWC will consult with WFO Guam regarding all tropical cyclones affecting Micronesia and Guam. Consultation will occur prior to issuing initial and final advisories and prior to issuing any advisory that indicates a significant change in forecast intensity or track from the previous advisory.
- Initiate, monitor, and update satellite invest areas on the tropical cyclone satellite websites provided by the Fleet Numerical Meteorology and Oceanography Center (FNMOC) and the Naval Research Laboratory (NRL), Monterey, California. NHC and CPHC will coordinate with JTWC on the initiation of desired invest areas and will provide JTWC numbers for invest areas as required.
- Deploy, through the Naval Oceanographic Office (NAVOCEANO), drifting data buoys in support of the Commander, U.S. Atlantic Fleet (COMLANTFLT) requirements.
- Consider the Tropical Cyclone Plan of the Day (TCPOD) as a request for assistance (RFA) from NOAA.
- At a minimum, maintain situation awareness of hurricane hunter operational missions conducted in applicable combatant command areas of responsibility.

2.4. **DOT and DHS Responsibilities**.

   2.4.1. Information Dissemination. The DOT will provide NWS with timely dissemination of significant information received regarding tropical and subtropical cyclones.

2.4.2. Flight Assistance. Through the Federal Aviation Administration (FAA), the DOT will provide air traffic control, communications, and flight assistance services.

2.4.3. U. S. Coast Guard. The Department of Homeland Security (DHS) will provide the following through the U.S. Coast Guard:

- Personnel, vessel, and communications support to the NDBC for development, deployment, and operation of moored environmental data buoy systems.
- Surface observations to NWS from selected coastal facilities and vessels.
- Communications circuits for relay of weather observations to NWS in selected areas.
- Coastal broadcast facilities at selected locations for tropical storm or hurricane forecasts and warnings.

2.5. <u>Annual Liaison with Other Nations</u>.

2.5.1. The DOD, DOC, and DOT will cooperate in arranging an annual trip to the Caribbean and the Gulf of Mexico area to carry out a continuing and effective liaison with the directors of meteorological services, air traffic control agencies, and disaster preparedness agencies of nations in those areas, regarding the provision of tropical cyclone warning services. Due to the international importance of this mission, the Air Force Reserve Command (AFRC) and NHC will jointly plan and execute this mission annually. The NHC will coordinate with the meteorological services in the countries to be visited.

2.5.2. This annual liaison trip is known as the Caribbean Hurricane Awareness Tour (CHAT). It takes place in the United States Southern and Northern Command's area of responsibility and supports their mission of promoting stability, collective security, and defending U.S. regional interests. The WC-130 aircraft flown by the 53rd Weather Reconnaissance Squadron (53rd WRS) "Hurricane Hunters" is the most visible symbol of this awareness program; it serves as an educational platform and as a media focus for both dignitaries and the local populace. Tours of the aircraft demonstrate the critical partnership between DOD and NOAA during the preparation of a tropical cyclone forecast. The CHAT increases public awareness of the hurricane threat and serves to recognize and strengthen national and international teamwork for storm warning and emergency response.

2.5.3. This diplomatic mission is unique in character and purpose. This joint AFRC and NOAA mission demonstrates the concerted U.S. effort to execute its hurricane program and illustrates the importance the U.S. places on hurricane forecasting, tracking, and warning. The CHAT helps communicate the U.S. responsibilities in the region and it highlights the vital roles of NOAA and 53rd WRS. The media's role is to document the trip and promote the hurricane preparedness message, thus providing visibility to this important outreach activity both nationally and internationally.

2.5.4. The synergy created by all participants traveling together on the 53rd WRS WC-130 aircraft is essential to efficiently accomplishing the overall objectives of the mission while exercising fiscal responsibility. AFRC may support the mission on a reimbursable, non-interference basis for: U.S. Department of Commerce (DOC) and National Oceanic and Atmospheric Administration (NOAA) staff, and other U.S. officials as appropriate. Media support may be provided within appropriate public affairs guidelines.

2.6. **Air Traffic Control/Flight Operations Coordination**. The operations officers of the principal flying units, the Manager, Air Traffic Control System Command Center (ATCSCC), Warrenton, VA, and the assistant managers for traffic management or assistant manager for military operations, as appropriate, at key Air Route Traffic Control Centers (ARTCC) will maintain a close working relationship on a continuing basis to ensure mission success under actual tropical storm conditions. This will involve visits to each other's facilities, familiarization flights, and telephone and electronic communications to improve the understanding of each other's requirements and capabilities.

2.6.1. Gulf of Mexico Weather Reconnaissance. The 53rd Weather Reconnaissance Squadron and the NOAA Aircraft Operations Center operations officers will maintain a close working relationship with the ATCSCC, the ARTCCs, and the Fleet Aerial Control and Surveillance Facility (FACSFAC) for the coordination of weather reconnaissance flights in the Gulf of Mexico and over the Caribbean Sea in particular, and in the United States in general. The operations officers will:

- Request the assistance of the appropriate ARTCC/FACSFAC in support of the National Hurricane Operations Plan.
- Provide the current operations officer's name and telephone number to the appropriate ARTCC and FACSFAC.
- Publish the unit's telephone numbers [Defense Switched Network (DSN)/Commercial]).

2.6.2. Air Traffic Control Assistance. The ATCSCC, appropriate ARTCCs, and FACSFAC will maintain a close working relationship with the weather reconnaissance units and provide airspace and air traffic control assistance to the extent possible. Those organizations will:

- Provide the current names and telephone numbers of points of contact to the flying units.
- Publish telephone numbers (DSN/Commercial).

CHAPTER 3

GENERAL OPERATIONS AND PROCEDURES OF THE
NATIONAL WEATHER SERVICE HURRICANE CENTERS

3.1. **General**. This chapter briefly describes the products, procedures, and communications headers used by the National Hurricane Center (NHC) and the Central Pacific Hurricane Center (CPHC). See Appendix A for a description of local National Weather Service (NWS) office products which support the tropical cyclone forecasting and warning program. Additional details of the products, including transmission times, can be found in National Weather Service Instruction 10-601, located at: http://www.weather.gov/directives.

3.2. **Products**.

      3.2.1. **Tropical Weather Outlook (TWO).** NHC and CPHC prepare the TWO during their respective tropical cyclone seasons. The outlook covers tropical and subtropical waters and discusses areas of disturbed weather and the potential for tropical cyclone development during the next 48 hours. The outlook will mention tropical cyclones and subtropical cyclones, including the system's location (in either general terms or map coordinates), status, and change in status.

      3.2.2. **Tropical Cyclone Public Advisories (TCP).** The TCP is the primary tropical cyclone information product issued to the public. The TCP comprises five sections: Summary, Watches and Warnings, Discussion and Outlook, Hazards, and Next Advisory. The NHC, the CPHC, and WFO Guam issue TCPs. The following pertains to the tropical storm/hurricane/typhoon watches and warnings contained in the TCP:

- NHC. NHC issues tropical storm/hurricane watches/warnings for the Atlantic, Pacific, and Gulf of Mexico coasts of the continental United States, the US Virgin Islands, and Puerto Rico. NHC issues watches when conditions along the coast are *possible* within 48 hours. NHC issues warnings when conditions along the coast are *expected* within 36 hours.

[NOTE: Because hurricane preparedness activities become difficult once winds reach tropical storm force, NHC issues the hurricane/typhoon watches *48 hours in advance of the anticipated onset of tropical-storm-force winds*.]

- CPHC and WFO Guam. CPHC and WFO Guam issues tropical storm/hurricane/typhoon watches/warnings for the islands of Hawaii, northwest Hawaiian Islands, Johnston Atoll, Guam, Northern Mariana Islands and selected points in the Micronesian countries. CPHC and WFO Guam issue watches when conditions along the coast are *possible* within 48 hours. CPHC and WFO Guam issue warnings when conditions are *expected* along the coast within 36 and 24 hours, respectively.

[NOTE: Because hurricane/typhoon preparedness activities become difficult once winds reach tropical storm force, CPHC and WFO Guam issue the hurricane/typhoon watches *48 hours in advance of the anticipated onset of <u>tropical-storm-force winds</u>*.]

Intermediate public advisories will be issued in between scheduled or special advisories when watches or warnings are in effect. They will continue to be issued when a tropical storm or hurricane is inland, even after coastal watches/warnings have been discontinued. These will retain the number of the last advisory they update plus an alphabetic designator (e.g., HURRICANE ALLISON INTERMEDIATE ADVISORY NUMBER 20A).

3.2.3. Tropical Cyclone Forecast/Advisories (TCM). NHC and CPHC will prepare TCMs for all tropical cyclones within their area of responsibility. See Section 4.3 for content and format of the advisories. The TCM provides critical tropical cyclone watch, warning, and forecast information for the protection of life and property.

[Note: In the Western Pacific, tropical cyclone forecasts/advisories are issued by the JTWC. Appendix C provides a listing of the abbreviated communications headings and titles for JTWC products. Information on the broadcast of tropical cyclone information to coastal and high-seas shipping can be found in Chapter 10, Marine Weather Broadcasts.]

3.2.4. Tropical Cyclone Discussions (TCD). The TCD is a primary tropical cyclone product explaining forecaster's reasoning behind analysis and the forecast for a tropical cyclone. It also provides coordinated 12-, 24-, 36-, 48-, 72-, 96-, and 120-hour tropical cyclone forecast positions and maximum sustained wind speed forecasts; other meteorological decisions; and plans for watches and warnings.

3.2.5. Tropical Cyclone Updates (TCU). TCUs are issued to inform users of significant changes in a tropical cyclone in between regularly scheduled public advisories. Such uses include, but are not limited to the following: to provide timely information of an unusual nature, such as the time and location of landfall, or to announce an expected change in intensity that results in an upgrade or downgrade of status (e.g., from a tropical storm to a hurricane); to provide a continuous flow of information regarding the center location of a tropical cyclone when watches or warnings are in effect and the center can be easily tracked with land-based radar; to provide advance notice that significant changes to storm information will be conveyed shortly, either through a subsequent TCU or through a Special Advisory; to announce changes to international watches or warnings made by other countries, or to cancel U.S. watches or warnings; or to issue a U.S. watch or warning, but only if the TCU precedes a special advisory that will contain the same watch/warning information, and indicates the special advisory will be issued shortly.

The TCU is a brief alphanumeric text product containing either block paragraph text, a formatted storm summary section, or both. The storm summary section is identical in format to the storm summary section found in the TCP. The storm summary section is required whenever the TCU is issued to update storm intensity, location, or motion information. The storm summary section is not required for TCUs issued to provide advance notice that significant changes to storm information will be conveyed shortly, or for those issued to convey changes to watches or warnings. TCUs issued to provide hourly storm location information will contain a headline indicating the purpose of the TCU (e.g., "...11 AM POSITION UPDATE...").

3.2.6. Tropical Cyclone Estimates (TCE). DELETED; previous data included in TCEs is incorporated in TCUs.

3.2.7. Graphical Tropical Cyclone Surface Wind Speed Probabilities. This graphical product portrays probabilistic surface wind speed information which will help users prepare for the potential of tropical storm or hurricane conditions. This product shows probabilities for three wind speed thresholds: 34, 50 and 64 knots. It provides cumulative probabilities through each 12 hour interval (e.g. 0 -12 hours, 0- 24 hours, etc.) from 0 through 120 hours. They are available in graphical forms in a static and an animated display. These wind speed probabilities are based on the track, intensity, and wind structure uncertainties in the official forecasts from the tropical cyclone centers.

3.2.8. Tropical Cyclone Surface Wind Speed Probabilities Text Product (PWS). This product portrays probabilistic wind speed information helping users prepare for the potential of tropical storm or hurricane conditions.

The probabilities in this product are statistically based on the errors in the official track and intensity forecasts issued during the past five years by NHC and CPHC. Variability in tropical cyclone wind structure is also incorporated. New probability values are computed for each new official forecast issued by NHC or CPHC.

The first section of the product provides categorical maximum wind speed (intensity) probabilities at standard forecast hours (12, 24, 36, 48, 72, 96, and 120) for various intensity stages (dissipated, tropical depression, tropical storm and hurricane) and for the five categories on the Saffir-Simpson Hurricane Wind Scale. These probabilities apply to the maximum sustained surface wind associated with the cyclone, and not to winds that could occur at specific locations.

Probabilities for specific locations are provided in the second section for sustained wind speeds equal to or exceeding three wind speed thresholds: 34, 50 and 64 knots. Two types of probability values are provided in this table: individual period and cumulative. Individual period probabilities are provided for each of the following time intervals: 0-12 hours, 12-24 hours, 24-36 hours, 36-48 hours, 48-72 hours, 72-96 hours, and 96-120 hours. These individual period probabilities indicate the chance that the particular wind speed will *start* during each individual period at each location. Cumulative probabilities are produced for the following time periods: 0-12 hours, 0-24 hours, 0-36 hours, 0-48 hours, 0-72 hours, 0-96 hours, and 0-120 hours. These cumulative probabilities indicate the overall chance the particular wind speed will occur at each location during the period between hour 0 and the forecast hour.

3.2.9. Tropical Cyclone Watch Warning Product (TCV). The TCV summarizes all new, continued, and cancelled tropical cyclone watches and warnings issued by the NHC for the U.S. Atlantic and Gulf coast, southern California coast, Puerto Rico, and U.S. Virgin Islands. The CPHC will issue a TCV for the main islands of the State of Hawaii. The product is issued each time a U. S. tropical cyclone watch and/or warning is issued, continued, or discontinued for all Atlantic, portions of the North East Pacific, and the North Central Pacific Ocean basin tropical cyclones.

3.2.10. Weather Prediction Center (WPC) Public Advisories (TCP). The National Centers for Environmental Prediction's WPC issues public advisories after NHC discontinues its advisories on subtropical and tropical cyclones that have moved inland in the conterminous United States or Mexico, but still pose a threat of heavy rain and flash floods in the conterminous United States or Mexico. The last NHC advisory will normally be issued when winds in an inland tropical cyclone drop below tropical storm strength, and the tropical depression is not forecast to regain tropical storm intensity or re-emerge over water. Therefore WPC will only handle tropical depressions or remnants. WPC advisories will terminate when the threat of flash flooding has ended.

3.2.11. Other Tropical Cyclone Products. Several other tropical cyclone related products are issued to support the tropical cyclone forecasting and warning program. Refer to NWS Instruction 10-601, located at http://www.weather.gov/directives, for further details on these products, which include:
- Satellite Interpretation Message (SIM).
- Tropical Weather Discussion (TWD).
- Tropical Weather Summary (TWS).
- Tropical Cyclone Summary – Fixes (TCS).
- Tropical Cyclone Danger Area Graphic
- Aviation Tropical Cyclone Advisory (TCA)
- Tropical Cyclone Reports (TCR)
- Tropical Cyclone Track and Watch/Warning Graphic
- Cumulative Wind Distribution
- Tropical Cyclone Surface Wind Field Graphic
- Maximum Wind Speed Probability Table
- Tropical Cyclone Storm Surge Probabilities

3.2.12. NHC and CPHC Continuance of Advisories and Products for Post-Tropical Cyclones. The NHC and CPHC will continue issuing advisory products after a tropical cyclone becomes post-tropical in those cases where the system continues to pose a significant threat to life and property and where the transfer or responsibility to another office would result in an unacceptable discontinuity of service. Similarly, WFO Guam will continue issuing advisory products after a tropical cyclone becomes post-tropical in those cases where the system continues to pose a significant threat to life and property.

3.3.   Numbering and Naming of Tropical and Subtropical Cyclones. The hurricane centers will number tropical depressions in their areas of responsibility. Depression numbers are always spelled out (e.g., "ONE," "TWO," "THREE," etc.). Depression numbers are assigned to match the seasonal cyclone number, even if a previous cyclone has bypassed the depression stage. For example, if the first tropical cyclone of the season forms directly as a storm (e.g., a fast-moving tropical wave becomes a tropical storm without ever becoming a depression), then the depression number "ONE" would simply be skipped and not used until the following year. For ease in differentiation, tropical depression numbers shall include the suffix "E" for Eastern Pacific, "C" for Central Pacific, or "W" for Western Pacific, after the number.

In both the Atlantic and Pacific, once the depression has reached tropical storm intensity, it shall be named and the depression number dropped. The depression number will not be used again until the following year. Give tropical cyclones a name in the first advisory after intensifying to 34 knots (39 mph) or greater. In the Western Pacific, WFO Guam will use the JTWC cyclone number for all non-named systems. For RSMC Tokyo named systems, WFO Guam will use the RSMC Tokyo name with the associated JTWC number in parentheses.

The following rules apply for tropical cyclones passing from one basin to another: Retain the name if a tropical cyclone passes from one basin into another basin as a tropical cyclone; i.e., advisories are continuous. An unnamed tropical depression will also retain its number (e.g. Tropical Depression Six-E remains Tropical Depression Six-E) if it crosses into another area of responsibility. For unnamed tropical depressions moving from west to east across 180°, CPHC will use the associated Joint Typhoon Warning Center's (JTWC) number and indicate JTWC in parentheses following the number. For named systems, CPHC will use the associated RSMC Tokyo name and provide the associated JTWC number in parentheses.

Within a basin, if the remnant of a tropical cyclone redevelops into a tropical cyclone, it is assigned its original number or name. If the remnants of a former tropical cyclone regenerate in a new basin, the regenerated tropical cyclone will be given a new designation.

3.3.1. Atlantic Basin. Depression numbers, ONE, TWO, THREE, will be assigned by the NHC after advising the Fleet Weather Center, Norfolk. Annual lists of Atlantic storm names are provided in Table 3-1.

3.3.2. Pacific East of 140°W. Depression numbers, with the suffix E, e.g., ONEE, TWOE, THREEE, will be assigned by the NHC after advising JTWC, Pearl Harbor, HI. The assigned identifier shall be retained even if the depression passes into another warning area. Annual lists of Eastern Pacific storm names are provided in Table 3-2.

3.3.3. Pacific West of 140°W and East of 180°. Depression numbers, with suffix C; e.g., ONEC, TWOC, THREEC, will be assigned by the CPHC after advising JTWC. Rotating lists of Central Pacific storm names are provided in Table 3-3.

3.3.4. Pacific West of 180° and North of 0°. Depression numbers, with suffix W; e.g., ONE-W, TWO-W, THREE-W, are assigned by JTWC. Rotating lists of Western Pacific storm names are provided in Table 3-4.

3.3.5. Subtropical Depressions. A single list of numbers and names will be used for all tropical and subtropical cyclones in each basin. Therefore, numbering of subtropical depressions will follow the same procedure as tropical depressions. For example, if the first subtropical depression follows the first tropical depression, the subtropical depression will be given the designation SUBTROPICAL DEPRESSION TWO. If a subtropical depression becomes a subtropical storm, it receives the next available name in the tropical cyclone naming sequence.

3.4. Transfer of Warning Responsibility.

3.4.1. NHC to CPHC. When a tropical or subtropical cyclone approaches 140°W, the coordinated transfer of warning responsibility from NHC to CPHC will be made and the appropriate advisory issued.

3.4.2. CPHC to JTWC/(RSMC, Tokyo)/WFO Guam. When a tropical or subtropical cyclone crosses 180° from east to west, the coordinated transfer of warning responsibility from CPHC to JTWC will be made and the appropriate advisory issued. At the same time, the CPHC will coordinate with the RSMC, Tokyo and WFO Guam so that they are aware that CPHC will be suspending the issuance of advisories.

3.4.3. JTWC/RSMC, Tokyo to CPHC. When a tropical or subtropical cyclone crosses 180° from west to east, the coordinated transfer of warning responsibility from JTWC to CPHC will be made. At the same time, the CPHC will coordinate with RSMC, Tokyo so that they are aware that CPHC will be assuming the issuance of advisories.

3.5. Alternate Warning Responsibilities.

3.5.1. Transfer to Alternate. In the event of impending or actual operational failure of a hurricane forecast center, tropical warning responsibilities will be transferred to an alternate facility in accordance with existing directives and retained there until resumption of responsibility can be made. Alternate facilities are as follows:

PRIMARY	ALTERNATE
NHC	Atlantic Basin: National Centers for Environmental Prediction Weather Prediction Center (WPC), College Park, MD Eastern Pacific Basin: CPHC
CPHC	NHC
CARCAH	53rd Weather Reconnaissance Squadron (53 WRS)
JTWC	Fleet Numerical Meteorology and Oceanography Center (FLENUMETOCCEN), Monterey, CA
WFO Guam	CPHC

3.5.2. Notification. The Fleet Weather Center, Norfolk, and JTWC, Pearl Harbor, will be advised by NHC, CARCAH, and CPHC, as appropriate, of impending or actual transfer of responsibility by the most rapid means available. JTWC will advise CPHC, NHC, and WFO Guam of impending or actual transfer of JTWC responsibilities. In the event of a CARCAH operational failure, direct communication is authorized between the 53 WRS and the forecast facility. Contact 53 WRS at DSN 597-2409/228-377-2409 or through the Keesler AFB Command Post at DSN 597-4181/4330; COM 228-377-4181/4330 (ask for the 53 WRS).

Table 3-1. Atlantic Tropical Cyclone Names

2014		2015		2016	
Name	**Pronunciation**	**Name**	**Pronunciation**	**Name**	**Pronunciation**
Arthur	AR-thur	Ana	AH-nah	Alex	AL-leks
Bertha	BUR-thuh	Bill	bill	Bonnie	BAH-nee
Cristobal	krees-TOH-bahl	Claudette	klaw-DET	Colin	KAH-lihn
Dolly	DAH-lee	Danny	DAN-ee	Danielle	dan-YELL
Edouard	eh-DWARD	Erika	eh-RIH-kuh	Earl	URR-ull
Fay	fay	Fred	frehd	Fiona	fee-OH-nuh
Gonzalo	gohn- SAH-loh	Grace	grayss	Gaston	ga-STAWN
Hanna	HAN-uh	Henri	ahn-REE	Hermine	her-MEEN
Isaias	ees-ah-EE-ahs	Ida	EYE-duh	Ian	EE-an
Josephine	JOH-seh-feen	Joaquin	wah-KEEN	Julia	JOO-lee-uh
Kyle	KY-ull	Kate	kayt	Karl	KAR-ull
Laura	LOOR-ruh	Larry	LAIR-ree	Lisa	LEE-suh
Marco	MAR-koe	Mindy	MIN-dee	Matthew	MATH-yoo
Nana	NA-na	Nicholas	NIH-kuh-luss	Nicole	nih-KOHL
Omar	OH-mar	Odette	oh-DEHT	Otto	AHT-toh
Paulette	pawl-LET	Peter	PEE-tur	Paula	PAHL-luh
Rene	re-NAY	Rose	rohz	Richard	RIH-churd
Sally	SAL-ee	Sam	sam	Shary	SHAHR-ee
Teddy	TEHD-ee	Teresa	tuh-REE-suh	Tobias	toh-BEE-uss
Vicky	VIH-kee	Victor	VIK-tur	Virginie	vir-JIN-ee
Wilfred	WILL-fred	Wanda	WAHN-duh	Walter	WALL-tur

2017		2018		2019	
Name	**Pronunciation**	**Name**	**Pronunciation**	**Name**	**Pronunciation**
Arlene	ar-LEEN	Alberto	al-BAIR-toe	Andrea	AN-dree-uh
Bret	bret	Beryl	BEHR-ril	Barry	BAIR-ree
Cindy	SIN-dee	Chris	kris	Chantal	shahn-TAHL
Don	dahn	Debby	DEH-bee	Dorian	DOR-ee-an
Emily	EH-mih-lee	Ernesto	er-NES-toh	Erin	AIR-rin
Franklin	FRANK-lin	Florence	FLOOR-ence	Fernand	fair-NAHN
Gert	gert	Gordon	GOR-duhn	Gabrielle	ga-bree-ELL
Harvey	HAR-vee	Helene	heh-LEEN	Humberto	oom-BAIR-toh
Irma	ER-mah	Isaac	EYE-zik	Imelda	ee-MEHL-dah
Jose	ho-ZAY	Joyce	joyss	Jerry	JEHR-ee
Katia	KAH-tyah	Kirk	kurk	Karen	KAIR-ren
Lee	lee	Leslie	LEHZ-lee	Lorenzo	loh-REN-zoh
Maria	ma-REE-ah	Michael	MY-kuhl	Melissa	meh-LIH-suh
Nate	nait	Nadine	nay-DEEN	Nestor	NES-tor
Ophelia	o-FEEL-ya	Oscar	AHS-kur	Olga	OAL-guh
Philippe	fee-LEEP	Patty	PAT-ee	Pablo	PAHB-lo
Rina	REE-nuh	Rafael	rah-fah--ELL	Rebekah	reh-BEH-kuh
Sean	shawn	Sara	SAIR-uh	Sebastien	suh-BASH-chuhn
Tammy	TAM-ee	Tony	TOH-nee	Tanya	TAHN-yuh
Vince	vinss	Valerie	VAH-lur-ee	Van	van
Whitney	WHIT-nee	William	WILL-yum	Wendy	WEN-dee

[Note: If over 21 tropical cyclones occur in a year, the Greek alphabet will be used following the W-named cyclone.]

Table 3-2. Eastern Pacific Tropical Cyclone Names

2014 Name	Pronunciation	2015 Name	Pronunciation	2016 Name	Pronunciation
Amanda	uh-MAN-duh	Andres	ahn-DRASE	Agatha	A-guh-thuh
Boris	bor-EES	Blanca	BLAHN-kah	Blas	blahs
Cristina	kris-TEE-nuh	Carlos	KAR-loess	Celia	SEEL-yuh
Douglas	DUG-luss	Dolores	deh-LOOR-ess	Darby	DAR-bee
Elida	ELL-ee-dah	Enrique	ahn-REE-kay	Estelle	eh-STELL
Fausto	FOW-sto	Felicia	fa-LEE-sha	Frank	frank
Genevieve	jeh-nuh-VEEV	Guillermo	gee-YER-mo	Georgette	jor-JET
Hernan	her-NAHN	Hilda	HILL-duh	Howard	HOW-urd
Iselle	ee-SELL	Ignacio	eeg-NAH-see-oh	Isis	EYE-sis
Julio	HOO-lee-o	Jimena	he-MAY-na	Javier	hahv-YAIR
Karina	kuh-REE-nuh	Kevin	KEH-vin	Kay	kay
Lowell	LO-uhl	Linda	LIHN-duh	Lester	LESS-tur
Marie	muh-REE	Marty	MAR-tee	Madeline	MAD-eh-luhn
Norbert	NOR-bert	Nora	NOOR-ruh	Newton	NOO-tuhn
Odile	oh-DEAL	Olaf	OH-lahf	Orlene	or-LEEN
Polo	POH-loh	Patricia	puh-TRIH-shuh	Paine	payne
Rachel	RAY-chull	Rick	rik	Roslyn	RAWZ-luhn
Simon	SY-muhn	Sandra	SAN-druh	Seymour	SEE-mor
Trudy	TROO-dee	Terry	TAIR-ree	Tina	TEE-nuh
Vance	vanss	Vivian	VIH-vee-uhn	Virgil	VUR-jill
Winnie	WIN-ee	Waldo	WAHL-doh	Winifred	WIN-ih-fred
Xavier	ZAY-vee-ur	Xina	ZEE-nah	Xavier	ZAY-vee-ur
Yolanda	yo-LAHN-da	York	york	Yolanda	yo-LAHN-da
Zeke	zeek	Zelda	ZEL-dah	Zeke	zeek

2017 Name	Pronunciation	2018 Name	Pronunciation	2019 Name	Pronunciation
Adrian	AY-dree-uhn	Aletta	a-LET-ah	Alvin	AL-vin
Beatriz	BEE-a-triz	Bud	buhd	Barbara	BAR-bruh
Calvin	KAL-vin	Carlotta	kar-LOT-uh	Cosme	COS-may
Dora	DOR-ruh	Daniel	DAN-yuhl	Dalila	dah-LY-lah
Eugene	YOU-jeen	Emilia	ee-MILL-ya	Erick	EHR-ik
Fernanda	fer-NAN-dah	Fabio	FAH-bee-o	Flossie	FLOSS-ee
Greg	greg	Gilma	GIL-mah	Gil	gill
Hilary	HIH-luh-ree	Hector	HEHK-tor	Henriette	hen-ree-ETT
Irwin	UR-win	Ileana	ill-ay-AH-nah	Ivo	eye-VOH
Jova	HO-vah	John	jahn	Juliette	jew-lee-EHT
Kenneth	KEH-neth	Kristy	KRIS-tee	Kiko	KEE-ko
Lidia	LIH-dyah	Lane	layne	Lorena	low-RAY-na
Max	maks	Miriam	MEER-yim	Mario	MAR-ee-o
Norma	NOOR-muh	Norman	NOR-muhn	Narda	NAHR-duh
Otis	OH-tis	Olivia	uh-LIV-ee-uh	Octave	AHK-tayv
Pilar	Pee-LAHR	Paul	pall	Priscilla	prih-SIH-luh
Ramon	rah-MOHN	Rosa	ROH-zuh	Raymond	RAY-mund
Selma	SELL-mah	Sergio	SIR-gee-oh	Sonia	SOHN-yah
Todd	tahd	Tara	TAIR-uh	Tico	TEE-koh
Veronica	vur-RAHN-ih-kuh	Vicente	vee-CEN-tay	Velma	VELL-muh
Wiley	WY-lee	Willa	WIH-lah	Wallis	WAHL-lis
Xina	ZEE-nah	Xavier	ZAY-vee-ur	Xina	ZEE-nah
York	york	Yolanda	yo-LAHN-da	York	york
Zelda	ZEL-dah	Zeke	zeek	Zelda	ZEL-dah

Table 3-3. Central Pacific Tropical Cyclone Names

COLUMN 1		COLUMN 2	
Name	**Pronunciation**	**Name**	**Pronunciation**
AKONI	ah-KOH-nee	AKA	AH-kah
EMA	EH-mah	EKEKA	eh-KEH-kak
HONE	HOH-neh	HENE	HEH-neh
IONA	ee-OH-nah	IOLANA	ee-OH-lah-nah
KELI	KEH-lee	KEONI	keh-ON-nee
LALA	LAH-lah	LINO	LEE-noh
MOKE	MOH-keh	MELE	MEH-leh
NOLO	NOH-loh	NONA	NOH-nah
OLANA	Oh-LAH-nah	OLIWA	oh-LEE-vah
PENA	PEH-nah	PAMA	PAH-mah
ULANA	oo-LAH-nah	UPANA	oo-PAH-nah
WALE	WAH-leh	WENE	WEH-neh
COLUMN 3		**COLUMN 4**	
Name	**Pronunciation**	**Name**	**Pronunciation**
ALIKA	ah-LEE-kah	ANA	AH-nah
ELE	EH-leh	ELA	EH-lah
HUKO	HOO-koh	HALOLA	hah-LOH-lah
IOPA	ee-OH-pah	IUNE	ee-OO-neh
KIKA	KEE-kah	KILO	KEE-lo
LANA	LAH-nah	LOKE	LOH-keh
MAKA	MAH-kah	MALIA	mah-LEE-ah
NEKI	NEH-kee	NIALA	nee-AH-lah
OMEKA	oh-MEH-kah	OHO	OH-hoh
PEWA	PEH-vah	PALI	PAH-lee
UNALA	oo-NAH-lah	ULIKA	oo-LEE-kah
WALI	WAH-lee	WALAKA	wah-LAH-kah

[Note: Use Column 1 list of names until exhausted before going to Column 2, etc. All letters in the Hawaiian language are pronounced, including double or triple vowels.]

Table 3-4. International Tropical Cyclone Names for the Northwest Pacific and South China Sea

Contributor	I	II	III	IV	V
	NAME	NAME	NAME	NAME	NAME
Cambodia	Damrey	Kong-rey	Nakri	Krovanh	Sarika
China	Longwang	Yutu	Fengshen	Dujuan	Haima
DPR Korea	Kirogi	Toraji	Kalmaegi	Maemi	Meari
HK, China	Kai-tak	Man-yi	Fung-wong	Choi-wan	Ma-on
Japan	Tembin	Usagi	Kammuri	Koppu	Tokage
Lao PDR	Bolaven	Pabuk	Phanfone	Ketsana	Nock-ten
Macau	Chanchu	Wutip	Vongfong	Parma	Muifa
Malaysia	Jelawat	Sepat	Nuri	Melor	Merbok
Micronesia	Ewiniar	Fitow	Sinlaku	Nepartak	Nanmadol
Philippines	Bilis	Danas	Hagupit	Lupit	Talas
RO Korea	Kaemi	Nari	Changmi	Sudal	Noru
Thailand	Prapiroon	Wipha	Mekkhala	Nida	Kulap
U.S.A.	Maria	Francisco	Higos	Omais	Roke
Viet Nam	Saomai	Lekima	Bavi	Conson	Sonca
Cambodia	Bopha	Krosa	Maysak	Chanthu	Nesat
China	Wukong	Haiyan	Haishen	Dianmu	Haitang
DPR Korea	Sonamu	Podul	Pongsona	Mindulle	Nalgae
HK, China	Shanshan	Lingling	Yanyan	Tingting	Banyan
Japan	Yagi	Kajiki	Kujira	Kompasu	Washi
Lao PDR	Xangsane	Faxai	Chan-hom	Namtheun	Matsa
Macau	Bebinca	Peipan	Linfa	Malou	Sanvu
Malaysia	Rumbia	Tapah	Nangka	Meranti	Mawar
Micronesia	Soulik	Mitag	Soudelor	Rananim	Guchol
Philippines	Cimaron	Hagibis	Molave	Malakas	Talim
RO Korea	Chebi	Noguri	Koni	Megi	Nabi
Thailand	Durian	Rammasun	Morakot	Chaba	Khanun
U.S.A.	Utor	Matmo	Etau	Aere	Vicente
Viet Nam	Trami	Halong	Vamco	Songda	Saola

[NOTE: The official international name list was effective January 1, 2000. Names will be assigned in rotation starting with Damrey for the first tropical cyclone of the year 2000 which is of tropical storm strength or greater. When the last name in column 5 (Saola) is used, the sequence will begin again with the first name in column 1.]

3.6.　**Abbreviated Communications Headings**. Abbreviated communications headings are assigned to advisories on tropical and subtropical cyclones and other advisories based on depression numbers or storm name and standard communications procedures governed by the World Meteorological Organization (WMO). An abbreviated heading consists of three groups with ONE space between each of the groups. The first group contains a data type indicator (e.g., WT for hurricane), a geographical indicator (e.g. NT for Atlantic Basin), and a number. The second group contains a location identifier of the message originator (e.g., KNHC for NHC). The third group is a date-time group in UTC. An example of a complete header is: WTNT61 KNHC 180400. Table 3-5 provides the abbreviated communications headings for products issued by NHC, CPHC, and WFO Guam.

Table 3-5. Summary of Products and their Associated WMO Header

PRODUCT TITLE	WMO HEADER
Tropical Weather Outlook	
Atlantic Basin	ABNT20 KNHC
Eastern Pacific	ABPZ20 KNHC
Central Pacific	ACPN50 PHFO
Tropical Weather Discussion	
Atlantic Basin	AXNT20 KNHC
Eastern Pacific	AXPZ20 KNHC
Tropical/Subtropical Cyclone Public Advisory	
Atlantic Basin	WTNT31-35 KNHC
Eastern Pacific	WTPZ31-35 KNHC
Central Pacific	WTPA31-35 PHFO
Western Pacific	WTPQ31-35 PGUM
Tropical Cyclone Surface Wind Speed Probabilities Text Product	
Atlantic Basin	FONT11-15 KNHC
Eastern Pacific	FOPZ11-15 KNHC
Central Pacific	FOPA11-15 PHFO
Tropical/Subtropical Cyclone Forecast/Advisory	
Atlantic Basin	WTNT21-25 KNHC
Eastern Pacific	WTPZ21-25 KNHC
Central Pacific	WTPA21-25 PHFO
Tropical Cyclone Discussion	
Atlantic Basin	WTNT41-45 KNHC
Eastern Pacific	WTPZ41-45 KNHC
Central Pacific	WTPA41-45 PHFO
Tropical Cyclone Valid Time Event Code Product	
Atlantic Basin	WTNT81-85 KNHC
Eastern Pacific	WTPZ81-85 KNHC
Central Pacific	WTPA81-85 PHFO
Tropical Cyclone Update	
Atlantic Basin	WTNT61-65 KNHC
Eastern Pacific	WTPZ61-65 KNHC
Central Pacific	WTPA61-65 PHFO
Tropical Weather Summary	
Atlantic Basin	ABNT30 KNHC
Eastern Pacific	ABPZ30 KNHC
Central Pacific	ACPN60 PHFO

Table 3-5 (continued). Summary of Products and their Associated WMO Header

PRODUCT TITLE	WMO HEADER
Tropical Cyclone Position and Intensity from Satellite Data	
South Central Pacific 120W	TXPS40 PHFO
North Central Pacific 140W - 180	TXPN40 PHFO
Satellite Interpretation Message	
Hawaiian Islands	ATHW40 PHFO
West Pacific (Guam)	ATPQ40 PGUM
Satellite-Derived Rainfall	
Eastern Caribbean	TCCA21 KNHC
Central Caribbean	TCCA22 KNHC
Western Caribbean	TCCA23 KNHC
Aviation Tropical Cyclone Advisory Message	
Atlantic Basin	FKNT21-25 KNHC
Eastern Pacific	FKPZ21-25 KNHC
Central Pacific	FKPA21-25 PHFO
Tropical Cyclone Summary - Fixes	
South Central Pacific 120W	TXPS41-45 PHFO
North Central Pacific 140W - 180	TXPN41-45 PHFO

[Note: Refer to Appendix C for abbreviated communications headers and titles for the products for which JTWC is responsible.]

3.7. **Hurricane Liaison Team (HLT).** The HLT is a Department of Homeland Security's Federal Emergency Management Agency (FEMA)-sponsored team made up of federal, state, and local emergency managers who have extensive hurricane operational experience. Team members function as a bridge between scientists, meteorologists and the emergency managers who respond if the storm threatens the United States or its territories. Team members provide immediate and critical storm information to government agency decision makers at all levels to help them prepare for their response operations, which may include evacuations, sheltering, and mobilizing equipment. State and/or local officials, not the HLT, make decisions concerning evacuations.

3.7.1. **National Weather Service (NWS) Responsibilities.** The NWS supports the HLT through use of NHC meteorologists, Weather Forecast Office (WFO) personnel (typically warning coordination meteorologists and service hydrologists), and River Forecast Center (RFC) hydrologists. Eastern and Southern Region Headquarters will maintain a list of their available HLT candidates.

3.7.2. **Activation/Deployment.** On June 1st, or earlier if necessary, the NHC Director will request that the FEMA activate the HLT by contacting the Disaster Operations Directorate. The HLT will remain active throughout the season. When a tropical cyclone in the Atlantic or eastern North Pacific basins threatens the United States or its territories, the Director or Deputy Director of NHC may request NWS meteorological and/or hydrological support by contacting the appropriate NWS Regional Director. NWS personnel should deploy to NHC within 24 hours of the request for assistance.

NWS personnel will remain deployed at the HLT until the hurricane threat has passed. However, if a significant rainfall threat is expected to persist after landfall, the HLT will remain staffed by the FEMA to facilitate coordination with the Weather Prediction Center (WPC), who will assume briefing responsibilities until the rainfall threat has passed. NHC and WPC will coordinate the transfer of briefing responsibilities. During the inland event the HLT and WPC will coordinate with the appropriate WFOs and RFCs, and when needed, hydrologists from the RFCs will provide hydrological briefings.

If the HLT is deactivated, the WPC will assume the briefing duties provided the remnants of the tropical cyclone remain a threat to inland areas. NHC and WPC will coordinate prior to the transfer. During the inland event WPC will coordinate with the appropriate WFOs and RFCs and when needed, hydrologists from the RFCs will provide hydrological briefings.

3.7.3. Training. Completing NWS/FEMA's distance learning training module, Community Hurricane Preparedness, is required by HLT members. The module can be taken via the Internet at: http://meted.ucar.edu/hurrican/chp/index.htm. Other training opportunities are strongly encouraged. They are: FEMA's "Introduction to Hurricane Preparedness" conducted at NHC for emergency mangers and NWS personnel, and FEMA's annual HLT training session held at NHC.

3.7.4. Meteorological Duties. The HLT meteorologist will:
- Establish and maintain contact with the impacted WFOs, RFCs, and the WPC.
- Facilitate participation of the impacted NWS offices in conference calls, briefings, and in preparation and distribution of graphics.
- Provide meteorological interpretations on NHC advisories, WFO hurricane local statements, Hurrevac products, and storm surge forecasts for Federal, state and local agencies on request.
- Provide storm briefings via video/audio teleconferences for Federal, state and local organizations.
- Respond to meteorology-related incoming calls from Federal, state, and local emergency managers. Refer callers to the appropriate WFO for responses to localized special questions and issues.

3.7.5. Hydrologic Duties. The HLT hydrologist will:
- Establish and maintain contact with the impacted local WFOs, RFCs, and the WPC.
- Facilitate participation of the impacted NWS offices in conference calls, briefings, and in preparation and distribution of graphics.
- Provide hydrologic interpretation on NHC advisories, WFO hurricane local statements, and WFO and RFC hydrologic products for Federal, state and local agencies on request.
- Provide technical support for RFC lead during hydrologic portion of video teleconference. In absence of the RFC, lead the hydrologic portion of the video teleconference.
- Respond to hydrology-related incoming calls from Federal, state, and local emergency managers. Refer callers to the appropriate WFO for responses to localized special questions and issues.

CHAPTER 4

NATIONAL WEATHER SERVICE
PRODUCTS FOR THE DEPARTMENT OF DEFENSE

4.1. <u>General</u>. The Department of Defense (DOD) and the Department of Commerce (DOC) weather forecasting, reconnaissance, and distribution agencies share technical information and some responsibilities. Mutually supportive relationships have developed over the years and have resulted in a mutual dependency. Due to the nature and distribution of DOD resources and operations, the DOD requires certain meteorological information beyond that available to the general public. Accordingly, the DOC provides DOD with special observations and advisories on tropical and subtropical storms threatening DOD resources or operations.

4.2. <u>Observations.</u> The National Hurricane Center (NHC) and Central Pacific Hurricane Center (CPHC) will make available to DOD all significant tropical and subtropical cyclone observations that they receive.

4.3. <u>Tropical Cyclone Forecast/Advisories.</u>

4.3.1. General. The NHC and CPHC will provide to DOD forecasts and related information for tropical and subtropical weather disturbances of depression intensity or greater. Forecasts will include location, movement, intensity, and dimension of the disturbances. Tropical cyclone forecast/advisories will be disseminated through the National Weather Service (NWS) communications facility at Suitland, MD, to the Weather Product Management and Distribution System (WPMDS) at the Air Force Weather Agency (AFWA), Offutt AFB, NE, for further relay to DOD agencies. The DOD forecasters, who must give advice concerning an imminent operational decision, may contact the appropriate hurricane center forecaster (see Chapter 2) when published tropical cyclone forecast/advisories require elaboration. Telephone numbers for the hurricane centers are in Appendix I.

4.3.2. Tropical Cyclone Forecast/Advisory Issue Frequency. The first tropical cyclone forecast/advisory will normally be issued when meteorological data indicate that a tropical or subtropical cyclone has formed. Subsequent advisories will be issued at 0300, 0900, 1500, and 2100 UTC from NHC and CPHC. The public advisories issued by the NWS Forecast Office (WFO) Guam, are issued 1 hour after the JTWC guidance. Advisories will continue to be issued until the system is classified below the depression intensity level. In addition, special forecasts will be issued whenever the following criteria are met:

- A significant change has occurred, requiring the issuance of a revised forecast package.
- Conditions require a hurricane or tropical storm watch or warning to be issued. Remarks stating the reason for the special forecast or the relocation will be mandatory in all special forecasts or advisories that include a relocated position.

4.3.3. Tropical Cyclone Forecast/Advisory Content. Tropical cyclone forecast/ advisories issued by the NHC and CPHC will contain appropriate information as shown in

Figure 4-1. The forecast will contain 12, 24, 36, 48, 72, 96, and 120-hour tropical cyclone forecast positions. A code string is appended at the end of the line "NWS NATIONAL HURRICANE CENTER MIAMI FL." This is the Automated Tropical Cyclone Forecasting (ATCF) System Storm Identification Character String recognized by the WMO for tracking and verification of tropical cyclones. The ATCF <Storm ID> is three spaces after "FL" and uses the following format:

NWS NATIONAL HURRICANE CENTER MIAMI FL   BBCCYYYY
where:

BB = Ocean Basin

> **AL** - North Atlantic basin...north of the Equator
> **SL** - South Atlantic basin...south of the Equator
> **EP** - North East Pacific basin...eastward of 140°W
> **CP** - North Central Pacific basin between the Dateline and 140°W
> **WP** -North West Pacific basin...westward of the Dateline
> **IO** - North Indian Ocean basin...north of the Equator between 40°E and 100°E
> **SH** - South Pacific Ocean Basin and South Indian Ocean basin

CC = Cyclone Number

Numbers 01 through 49 are reserved for tropical and subtropical cyclones. A cyclone number is assigned to each tropical or subtropical cyclone in each basin as it develops. The numbers are assigned in chronological order.

Numbers 50 through 79 are reserved for internal use by operational forecast centers.

Numbers 80 through 89 are reserved for training, exercises and testing.

Numbers 90 through 99 are reserved for tropical disturbances which have the potential to become tropical or subtropical cyclones. Although not required, the 90's should be assigned sequentially and reused throughout the calendar year.

YYYY = Four-digit year
This is the calendar year for the Northern Hemisphere. For the Southern Hemisphere, the year begins July 1, with calendar year plus one.

[Note: Tropical cyclone public advisories issued by the NHC, CPHC, and WFO Guam will contain appropriate information as shown in the example in Figure 4-2.]

4.3.3.1. Definition of Wind Radii by Quadrant. The working definition of the wind radius for a quadrant is: use the largest radius of that wind speed found in the quadrant. Example: NHC's quadrants are defined as NE (0°-90°), SE (90°-180°), SW (180°-270°), and NW (270°-360°). Given a maximum 34-knot radius of 150 nautical miles (nm) at 0°, 90 nm at 120°, and 40 nm at 260°, the following line would be carried in the forecast/advisory: 150NE 90SE 40SW 150NW.

4.3.3.2. Numbering of Tropical and Subtropical Cyclone Forecast/Advisories. All tropical cyclone forecast/advisories for each unique system in the Atlantic and Pacific will be numbered sequentially beginning with the number 1. Some examples are listed below:

Subtropical Depression ONE Forecast/Advisory Number 1
Tropical Depression ONE Forecast/Advisory Number 1
Tropical Depression ONE Forecast/Advisory Number 2
Tropical Storm Anita Forecast/Advisory Number 3
Hurricane (Typhoon) Anita Forecast/Advisory Number 4
Tropical Depression Anita Forecast/Advisory Number 5

```
ZCZC MIATCMAT4 ALL
TTAA00 KNHC DDHHMM

HURRICANE IKE FORECAST/ADVISORY NUMBER  42
NWS NATIONAL HURRICANE CENTER MIAMI FL   AL092008
1500 UTC THU SEP 11 2008

CHANGES IN WATCHES AND WARNINGS WITH THIS ADVISORY...

A HURRICANE WARNING HAS BEEN ISSUED FROM MORGAN CITY LOUISIANA TO BAFFIN BAY TEXAS.

A TROPICAL STORM WARNING HAS BEEN ISSUED FROM SOUTH OF BAFFIN BAY TO PORT MANSFIELD TEXAS.

SUMMARY OF WATCHES AND WARNINGS IN EFFECT...

A HURRICANE WARNING IS IN EFFECT FOR...
* MORGAN CITY LOUISIANA TO BAFFIN BAY TEXAS

A TROPICAL STORM WARNING IS IN EFFECT FOR...
* EAST OF MORGAN CITY TO THE MISSISSIPPI-ALABAMA BORDER...INCLUDING
THE CITY OF NEW ORLEANS AND LAKE PONTCHARTRAIN
* SOUTH OF BAFFIN BAY TO PORT MANSFIELD

HURRICANE CENTER LOCATED NEAR 25.5N  88.4W AT 11/1500Z
POSITION ACCURATE WITHIN  10 NM

PRESENT MOVEMENT TOWARD THE WEST-NORTHWEST OR 290 DEGREES AT   9 KT

ESTIMATED MINIMUM CENTRAL PRESSURE  945 MB
MAX SUSTAINED WINDS  85 KT WITH GUSTS TO 105 KT.
64 KT......100NE 100SE  30SW  60NW.
50 KT......150NE 150SE  90SW 140NW.
34 KT......230NE 240SE 150SW 180NW.
12 FT SEAS..330NE 240SE 240SW 400NW.
WINDS AND SEAS VARY GREATLY IN EACH QUADRANT.  RADII IN NAUTICAL
MILES ARE THE LARGEST RADII EXPECTED ANYWHERE IN THAT QUADRANT.

REPEAT...CENTER LOCATED NEAR 25.5N  88.4W AT 11/1500Z
AT 11/1200Z CENTER WAS LOCATED NEAR 25.3N  88.0W

FORECAST VALID 12/0000Z 25.9N  90.0W
MAX WIND  90 KT...GUSTS 110 KT.
64 KT...100NE 100SE  30SW  60NW.
50 KT...150NE 150SE  90SW 140NW.
34 KT...230NE 240SE 150SW 180NW.

FORECAST VALID 12/1200Z 26.6N  92.0W
MAX WIND  95 KT...GUSTS 115 KT.
64 KT...100NE 100SE  50SW  60NW.
50 KT...150NE 150SE  90SW 140NW.
34 KT...230NE 240SE 150SW 180NW.

FORECAST VALID 13/0000Z 27.8N  94.2W
MAX WIND 105 KT...GUSTS 130 KT.
64 KT...100NE 100SE  50SW  60NW.
50 KT...150NE 150SE  90SW 120NW.
34 KT...230NE 240SE 150SW 160NW.

FORECAST VALID 13/1200Z 29.5N  95.9W...INLAND
MAX WIND 100 KT...GUSTS 120 KT.
50 KT...120NE 125SE  75SW  90NW.
34 KT...180NE 240SE 120SW 120NW.

FORECAST VALID 14/1200Z 34.5N  94.0W...INLAND
MAX WIND  35 KT...GUSTS  45 KT.
34 KT... 75NE  75SE  50SW  50NW.

EXTENDED OUTLOOK. NOTE...ERRORS FOR TRACK HAVE AVERAGED NEAR 225 NM
ON DAY 4 AND 300 NM ON DAY 5...AND FOR INTENSITY NEAR 20 KT EACH DAY

OUTLOOK VALID 15/1200Z 38.0N  85.0W...POST-TROP/EXTRATROP
MAX WIND  25 KT...GUSTS  35 KT.

OUTLOOK VALID 16/1200Z...ABSORBED

REQUEST FOR 3 HOURLY SHIP REPORTS WITHIN 300 MILES OF 25.5N  88.4W

NEXT ADVISORY AT 11/2100Z

$$
FORECASTER FRANKLIN
```

Figure 4-1. Tropical Cyclone Forecast/Advisory Format

[Note: NWS text products are limited to 69 characters per line. For the example above (Figure 4-1), there are more than 69 characters on some lines so the example could fit on one page.]

```
ZCZC MIATCPAT4 ALL
TTAA00 KNHC DDHHMM

BULLETIN
HURRICANE IKE ADVISORY NUMBER 42
NWS NATIONAL HURRICANE CENTER MIAMI FL   AL092008
1000 PM CDT THU SEP 11 2008

  IKE CONTINUES TO GROW IN SIZE BUT HAS NOT STRENGTHENED YET   HURRICANE WARNING ISSUED FOR NORTHWESTERN GULF COAST

SUMMARY OF 1000 PM CDT   0300 UTC   INFORMATION
---------------------------------------------
LOCATION   25 5N 88 4W
ABOUT 580 MI   930 KM ESE OF CORPUS CHRISTI TEXAS
ABOUT 470 MI   760 KM ESE OF GALVESTON TEXAS
MAXIMUM SUSTAINED WINDS   100 MPH   160 KM/HR
PRESENT MOVEMENT   WNW OR 290 DEGREES AT 10 MPH   17 KM/HR
MINIMUM CENTRAL PRESSURE   945 MB   27 91 INCHES

WATCHES AND WARNINGS
--------------------
CHANGES WITH THIS ADVISORY

A HURRICANE WARNING HAS BEEN ISSUED FROM MORGAN CITY LOUISIANA TO BAFFIN BAY TEXAS

A TROPICAL STORM WARNING HAS BEEN ISSUED FROM SOUTH OF BAFFIN BAY TO PORT MANSFIELD TEXAS

SUMMARY OF WATCHES AND WARNINGS IN EFFECT

A HURRICANE WARNING IS IN EFFECT FOR   MORGAN CITY LOUISIANA TO BAFFIN BAY TEXAS

A TROPICAL STORM WARNING IS IN EFFECT FOR   EAST OF MORGAN CITY TO THE MISSISSIPPI-ALABAMA BORDER   INCLUDING THE CITY OF NEW
ORLEANS AND LAKE PONTCHARTRAIN SOUTH OF BAFFIN BAY TO PORT MANSFIELD

A HURRICANE WARNING MEANS THAT HURRICANE CONDITIONS ARE EXPECTED SOMEWHERE WITHIN THE WARNING AREA   A WARNING IS TYPICALLY
ISSUED 36 HOURS BEFORE THE ANTICIPATED FIRST OCCURRENCE OF TROPICAL-STORM-FORCE WINDS   CONDITIONS THAT MAKE OUTSIDE PREPARATIONS
DIFFICULT OR DANGEROUS   PREPARATIONS TO PROTECT LIFE AND PROPERTY SHOULD BE RUSHED TO COMPLETION

A TROPICAL STORM WARNING MEANS THAT TROPICAL STORM CONDITIONS ARE EXPECTED SOMEWHERE WITHIN THE WARNING AREA WITHIN THE NEXT
36 HOURS

FOR STORM INFORMATION SPECIFIC TO YOUR AREA   INCLUDING POSSIBLE INLAND WATCHES AND WARNINGS   PLEASE MONITOR PRODUCTS ISSUED BY
YOUR LOCAL WEATHER OFFICE

DISCUSSION AND 48-HOUR OUTLOOK
------------------------------
AT 1000 PM CDT   0300Z   THE CENTER OF HURRICANE IKE WAS LOCATED NEAR LATITUDE 25 5 NORTH   LONGITUDE 88 4 WEST   IKE IS MOVING TOWARD
THE WEST-NORTHWEST NEAR 10 MPH   17 KM/HR   A GENERAL WEST- NORTHWESTWARD MOTION IS EXPECTED OVER THE NEXT DAY OR SO   AND THE
CENTER OF IKE SHOULD BE VERY NEAR THE COAST BY LATE FRIDAY

MAXIMUM SUSTAINED WINDS ARE NEAR 100 MPH   160 KM/HR   WITH HIGHER GUSTS   IKE IS A CATEGORY TWO HURRICANE ON THE SAFFIR-SIMPSON
SCALE   IKE IS FORECAST TO BECOME A MAJOR HURRICANE PRIOR TO REACHING THE COASTLINE

IKE REMAINS A VERY LARGE TROPICAL CYCLONE   HURRICANE FORCE WINDS EXTEND OUTWARD UP TO 115 MILES   185 KM   FROM THE CENTER   AND
TROPICAL STORM FORCE WINDS EXTEND OUTWARD UP TO 275 MILES   445 KM

THE LATEST MINIMUM CENTRAL PRESSURE REPORTED BY A NOAA HURRICANE HUNTER AIRCRAFT WAS 945 MB   27 91 INCHES

HAZARDS AFFECTING LAND
----------------------
STORM SURGE   STORM SURGE WILL RAISE WATER LEVELS AS MUCH AS 10 TO 15 FT ABOVE GROUND LEVEL ALONG THE COAST WITHIN THE HURRICANE
WARNING AREA   WITH LARGE AND DANGEROUS BATTERING WAVES   NEAR AND TO THE EAST OF WHERE THE CENTER OF IKE MAKES LANDFALL   STORM
SURGE WILL RAISE WATER LEVELS AS MUCH AS 5 TO 7 FEET ABOVE GROUND LEVEL ALONG THE COAST WITHIN THE TROPICAL STORM WARNING AREA
ALONG THE NORTHERN GULF COAST   THE SURGE   COULD PENETRATE AS FAR INLAND AS ABOUT 10 MILES FROM THE SHORE WITH DEPTH GRADUALLY
DECREASING AS THE WATER MOVES INLAND

WIND   BECAUSE IKE IS A VERY LARGE TROPICAL CYCLONE   WEATHER WILL DETERIORATE ALONG THE COASTLINE LONG BEFORE THE CENTER REACHES
THE COAST   HURRICANE CONDITIONS ARE EXPECTED TO REACH NORTHWESTERN GULF COAST WITHIN THE WARNING AREA FRIDAY AFTERNOON
WINDS ARE EXPECTED TO FIRST REACH TROPICAL STORM STRENGTH FRIDAY MORNING   MAKING OUTSIDE PREPARATIONS DIFFICULT OR DANGEROUS
PREPARATIONS TO PROTECT LIFE AND PROPERTY SHOULD BE RUSHED TO COMPLETION

RAINFALL   IKE IS EXPECTED TO PRODUCE RAINFALL AMOUNTS OF 5 TO 10 INCHES ALONG THE CENTRAL AND UPPER TEXAS COAST AND OVER PORTIONS
OF SOUTHWESTERN LOUISIANA   WITH ISOLATED MAXIMUM AMOUNTS OF 15 INCHES POSSIBLE   RAINFALL AMOUNTS OF 1 TO 2 INCHES ARE POSSIBLE
OVER PORTIONS OF THE YUCATAN PENINSULA


NEXT ADVISORY
-------------
NEXT INTERMEDIATE ADVISORY   100 AM CDT
NEXT COMPLETE ADVISORY   400 AM CDT

$$
FORECASTER FRANKLIN

NNNN
```

Figure 4-2. Tropical Cyclone Public Advisory Format

[Note: NWS text products are limited to 69 characters per line. For the example above (Figure 4-2), there are more than 69 characters on some lines so the example could fit on one page.]

CHAPTER 5

AIRCRAFT RECONNAISSANCE

5.1. <u>General</u>. All Department of Commerce (DOC) tropical and subtropical cyclone aircraft reconnaissance needs will be requested and provided in accordance with the procedures of this chapter. As outlined in the Air Force Reserve Command (AFRC)/National Oceanic and Atmospheric Administration (NOAA) Memorandum of Agreement (see Appendix F), DOC has identified a requirement for, and the Department of Defense (DOD) maintains aircraft to support, up to five sorties per day. Requirements exceeding five sorties will be accomplished on a "resources-permitting" basis. In times of national emergency or war, some or all DOD reconnaissance resources may not be available to fulfill DOC needs. The Global Decision Support System (GDSS) JCS Priority Code for tasked, operational weather reconnaissance is **1A3** (IAW DOD Regulation 4500.9-R and Joint Publications 4-01 and 4-04). The Force Activity Designator (FAD)/Urgency of Need Designator (UND) Supply Priority Designator Determination code is **IIA2** (IAW Joint Publication 4-01 and Air Force Manual 23-110, Volume 2, Part 13, Attachment 3A-2.)

5.2. <u>Responsibilities</u>. The DOD, through the AFRC's 53rd Weather Reconnaissance Squadron (53 WRS), and DOC, through NOAA's Aircraft Operations Center (AOC), operate a complementary fleet of aircraft to conduct hurricane/tropical cyclone reconnaissance, synoptic surveillance, and research missions.

5.2.1. DOD. The DOD is responsible for:

5.2.1.1. Providing operational aircraft for vortex fixes and data, synoptic surveillance missions, and investigative flights in response to DOC needs (see Figure 5-1).

5.2.1.2. Developing operational procedures and deploying data buoys to satisfy DOC needs.

5.2.2. DOC. The DOC is responsible for aircraft operations that may be requested to:

5.2.2.1. Provide synoptic surveillance soundings (see Figure 5-2).

5.2.2.2. Augment AFRC aircraft reconnaissance when DOC needs exceed the capabilities of DOD resources (see Figure 5-2).

5.2.2.3. Assume responsibility for hurricane reconnaissance over foreign airspace that may be restricted for military operations.

5.2.2.4. Conduct research flights.

5.2.3. DOT. The DOT is responsible for providing air traffic control services to aircraft when within airspace controlled by the FAA. This includes offshore oceanic airspace. Procedures for the expeditious handling of reconnaissance aircraft are documented in chapter 6, Airspace Operations.

Figure 5-1. WC-130J Weather Reconnaissance Aircraft

Figure 5-2. NOAA G-IV and WP-3D Weather Surveillance/Hurricane Aircraft

5.3. **Control of Aircraft.** Operational control of aircraft flying tropical and subtropical cyclone reconnaissance will remain with the operating agencies which own the aircraft.

5.4. Reconnaissance Requirements.

5.4.1. Meteorological Parameters.
Data needs in priority order are as follows:

- Geographical position of the flight level vortex center (vortex fix) and relative position of the surface center, if known.
- Wind data (continuous observations along the flight track) for surface and flight level.
- Center sea-level pressure determined by dropsonde or extrapolation from within 1,500 ft of the sea surface or from the computed 925 mb, 850 mb, or 700 mb height.
- Minimum 700, 850 or 925 mb height, if available.
- SFMR surface wind and rain rate.
- Radar reflectivity imagery.
- High density three-dimensional Doppler radial velocities of the tropical cyclone core circulation.
- Temperature at flight level.
- Sea-surface temperature.
- Dew-point temperature at flight level.

5.4.2. Accuracy.

5.4.2.1. Geographic Position.
- Aircraft position: within 3 nm.
- Storm surface center (wind/pressure): within 6 nm.
- Flight level storm center (wind/pressure): within 6 nm.

5.4.2.2. Wind Direction.
- Surface: within 10 deg.
- Flight level for winds greater than 20 kt: within 5 deg.

5.4.2.3. Wind Speed.
- Surface: within 10 kt.
- Flight level: within 4 kt.

5.4.2.4. Pressure Height.
- Surface: within 2 hPa.
- Flight level at or below 500 hPa: within 10 m.
- Flight level above 500 hPa: within 20 m.

5.4.2.5. Temperature.
- Sea surface: within 1°C.
- Flight level: within 1°C.

5.4.2.6. Dew-Point Temperature.
- From 20°C to +40°C: within 1°C.

- Less than 20°C: within 3°C.

5.4.2.7. Absolute Altitude: Within 10 m.

5.4.2.8. Vertical Sounding.
- Pressure: within 2 hPa.
- Temperature: within 1°C.
- Dew-point temperature:
- From 20°C to +40°C: within 1°C.
- Less than 20°C: within 3°C.
- Wind direction: within 10 deg.
- Wind speed: within 5 kt.

5.4.2.9. Core Doppler Radar.
- Horizontal resolution along aircraft track: 1.5 km
- Radar beam width: 3 degrees.
- Radar radial resolution (gate length): 150 m.
- Error in radar radial velocity: 1 m/s.
- Range: 50 km.

[NOTE: Present weather reconnaissance capabilities do not completely satisfy these requirements; data will be collected as close to stated requirements as possible.]

5.4.3. **High-Density/High-Accuracy (HD/HA) Data Requirements.** The HD/HA data include UTC time, aircraft latitude, longitude, static pressure, geopotential height, extrapolated sea level pressure or D-Value, air temperature, dew point temperature, flight-level (FL) wind direction, FL wind speed, peak 10-second (10-s) average FL wind speed, peak 10-s average surface wind speed from the stepped frequency microwave radiometer (SFMR), SFMR-derived rain rate, and quality control flags. Except for the peak values noted above, all data provided in HDOB messages are 30-second averages, regardless of the interval at which the HDOB messages are reported. See Appendix G for HDOB message formats. The DOC requires rapid acquisition and transmission of tropical cyclone data, especially within the 24-hour period prior to landfall. If HD/HA capability is lost on an operational mission, the airborne meteorologist will immediately contact Chief, Aerial Reconnaissance Coordination, All Hurricanes (CARCAH) to determine data requirements for the remainder of the mission.

5.4.4. **Synoptic Surveillance Data Requirements.** When required, NHC will request sounding data on the periphery of systems approaching the United States. NHC will provide specific tracks including control points, control times and dropwindsonde frequency allocations to CARCAH for coordination with the reconnaissance units.

5.4.5. **Core Doppler Radar Requirements.** When required, NHC and the Environmental Modeling Center (EMC) will coordinate to request high-density three-dimensional Doppler radial velocities in the tropical cyclone core for potential storms impacting the United States, including Puerto Rico and the Virgin Islands. EMC, NHC, and HRD will coordinate to provide specific flight plans to CARCAH for coordination with the reconnaissance units.

5.4.6. Required Frequency and Content of Observations. Observation requirements are summarized in Table 5-1. The inner core radar reflectivity would be provided at a rate of one image per Vortex Data Message and be sent within 30 minutes of transmission of the Vortex Data Message. Deviations to these requirements will be coordinated through CARCAH. The Vortex message format and information are shown in Figure 5-3, Figure 5-4, and Table 5-2. Other data message formats and code breakdowns can be found in Appendix G.

Table 5-1. Requirements for Aircraft Reconnaissance Data

	RECCO Section 1 plus 4ddff and 9VTTT as applicable	Vortex Data Message (VDM)	Vertical Data WMO Temp Drop Code (FM37-VII)	High Density Observation (HDOB)
En route	Approx. every 30 minutes over water not to exceed 200 nm	NA	Approx every 400 nm over water, or fewer/relocated per request or sonde conservation	30-sec interval
Invest area	At major turnpoints. Also, every 15 minutes if HDOBs are INOP.	After closing a circulation	NA	30-sec interval
Fix pattern	End points of Alpha pattern legs. When necessary with radar fix information.	Each fix.	Each tasked fix at or above 850 mb. Intermediate fixes and eyewall modules as requested.	30-sec interval

5.4.7. WP-3D Configuration. The minimum operational configuration of the WP-3D will include the stepped frequency microwave radiometer (SFMR), Doppler radar and the advanced vertical atmospheric profiling system (AVAPS).

5.5. Reconnaissance Planning and Flight Notification.

5.5.1. DOC Requests for Aircraft Reconnaissance Data.

5.5.1.1. Coordination. Any agency requesting aircraft reconnaissance (e.g., the NWS Environmental Modeling Center (EMC), the Central Pacific Hurricane Center (CPHC)) should contact the National Hurricane Center (NHC) no later than 1630 UTC the day prior to the requirement, and within the constraints of paragraph 5.5.2.1. NHC will compile the list of the total DOC requirements for data on tropical and subtropical cyclones or disturbances for the next 24-hour period (1100 to 1100 UTC) and an outlook for the succeeding 24-hour period. This coordinated request will be considered the agency's request for assistance (RFA) to DOD and will be provided to CARCAH as soon as possible, but no later than 1630 UTC each day in the format of Figure 5-5.

5.5.1.2. Tropical Cyclone Plan of the Day. From the coordinated DOC request, CARCAH will publish the Tropical Cyclone Plan of the Day (TCPOD). The format for the TCPOD is shown in Figure 5-6. When DOC reconnaissance needs exceed DOD and DOC resources, CARCAH will coordinate with the NHC to establish priorities of requirements.

DATE		SCHEDULED FIX TIME	AIRCRAFT NUMBER	ARWO	
WX MISSION IDENTIFICATION		STORM NUMBER IDENTIFIER			OB
VORTEX DATA MESSAGE					
A		DATE AND TIME OF FIX			
B	DEG MIN N S	LATITUDE OF VORTEX FIX			
	DEG MIN E W	LONGITUDE OF VORTEX FIX			
C		MINIMUM HEIGHT AT STANDARD LEVEL			
D		ESTIMATE OF MAXIMUM SURFACE WIND OBSERVED			
E		BEARING AND RANGE FROM CENTER OF MAXIMUM SURFACE WIND			
F		MAXIMUM FLIGHT LEVEL WIND NEAR CENTER			
G		BEARING AND RANGE FROM CENTER OF MAXIMUM FLIGHT LEVEL WIND			
H		MINIMUM SEA LEVEL PRESSURE COMPUTED FROM DROPSONDE OR EXTRAPOLATED FROM FLIGHT LEVEL. IF EXTRAPOLATED, CLARIFY IN REMARKS.			
I		MAXIMUM FLIGHT LEVEL TEMP/PRESSURE ALTITUDE OUTSIDE EYE			
J		MAXIMUM FLIGHT LEVEL TEMP/PRESSURE ALTITUDE INSIDE EYE			
K		DEWPOINT TEMP/SEA SURFACE TEMP INSIDE EYE			
L		EYE CHARACTER: Closed wall, poorly defined, open SW, etc.			
M		EYE SHAPE/ORIENTATION/DIAMETER. **CODE EYE SHAPE AS:** C -Circular; CO - Concentric; E- Elliptical. **TRANSMIT ORIENTATION OF MAJOR AXIS IN TENS OF DEGREE** (i.e., 01-010 to 190; 17-170 to 350). **TRANSMIT DIAMETER IN NAUTICAL MILES.** Examples: C8 - Circular eye 8 miles in diameter. EO9/15/5 - Elliptical eye, major axis 090-270, length of major axis 15 NM, length of minor axis 5NM. CO8-14 - Concentric eye, diameter inner eye 8 NM, outer eye 14 NM.			
N		FIX DETERMINED BY/FIX LEVEL. **FIX DETERMINED BY:** 1 - Penetration; 2 - Radar; 3 - Wind; 4 - Pressure; 5 - Temperature. **FIX LEVEL:** Indicate surface center if visible; indicate both surface and flight level centers only when same: 0 - Surface; 1 - 1500ft; 9-925mb; 8 - 850 mb; 7 - 700 mb; 5 - 500 mb; 4 - 400 mb; 3 - 300 mb; 2 - 200 mb; NA - Other.			
O		NAVIGATION FIX ACCURACY/METEOROLOGICAL ACCURACY			
P	REMARKS MAX FL WIND_____KT_____BEARING / RANGE NM_____Z MAX OUTBOUND FL WIND_____KT_____BEARING / RANGE NM_____Z MAX OUTBOUND AND MAX FL WIND ____ KT ____ BEARING / RANGE NM _____Z CNTR DROPSONDE SFC WIND _____/_____KT SLP EXTRAP FROM (Below 1500 FT/ 925 MB/ 850 MB/ 700 MB/ DROPSONDE) SFC CNTR_____/_____NM FROM FL CNTR MAX FL TEMP _____C_____/_____NM FROM FL CNTR SURFACE WIND OBSERVED VISUALLY				
INSTRUCTIONS: Items A through G (and H when extrapolated) are transmitted from the aircraft immediately following the fix. The remainder of the message is transmitted as soon as available.					

Figure 5-3. Vortex Data Message Worksheet

Table 5-2. Vortex Data Message Entry Explanation

DATA ITEM	ENTRY
Mission Identifier	As determined in Chapter 5, paragraph 5.7.6.
Storm Identifier	As determined in Chapter 4, paragraph 4.3.3.
Observation Number	A two digit number determined by the sequential order in which the observation is transmitted from the aircraft.
A (ALPHA)	Date and time (UTC) of the flight level center fix. If the flight level center cannot be fixed and the surface center is visible, enter the time of the surface center fix.
B (BRAVO)	The latitude and longitude of the center fix associated with item ALPHA. NOTE: If the surface center is fixable, enter bearing and range from the FL center in Remarks; e.g., SFC CNTR 270/15 nm, if the centers are separated by over 5 nm.
C (CHARLIE)	Indicate the standard atmospheric surface e.g. 925, 850 or 700 hPa. The minimum height of the standard surface observed inside the center. If at 1,500 ft or below or not within 1,500 ft of a standard surface, enter NA.
D (DELTA)	The maximum surface wind observed during the inbound leg associated with this fix. When SFMR surface wind data are unavailable, the surface wind is determined visually.
E (ECHO)	Bearing and range of the maximum surface wind observed (item DELTA) from the coordinates reported in item BRAVO.
F (FOXTROT)	The maximum flight level wind observed during the inbound leg associated with this fix. If a significant secondary maximum wind is observed, report it in remarks. All winds reported should be 10-s averages.
G (GOLF)	Bearing and range of the maximum flight level wind observed (item FOXTROT) from the coordinates reported in item BRAVO.
H (HOTEL)	The minimum sea level pressure (SLP) to the nearest millibar observed at the coordinates reported in item BRAVO. Preface the SLP with "EXTRAP" (extrapolated) when the data are not derived from dropsonde or when the SLP is extrapolated from a dropsonde that terminated early. Clarify the difference in remarks (e.g., "SLP EXTRAPOLATED FROM BELOW 1,500 FEET/925 MB/850 MB/700 MB/DROPSONDE").
I (INDIA)	MAX FLT LVL TEMP--This temperature is taken just outside the central region of a cyclone (i.e., just outside the eyewall or just beyond the maximum wind band). This temperature may not be the highest recorded on the inbound leg but is representative of the environmental temperature just outside the central region of the storm. PRESSURE ALT--Pressure altitude data (meters) are taken at the same location as the maximum temperature data reported in item INDIA.

Table 5-2 (continued). Vortex Data Message Entry Explanation

DATA ITEM	ENTRY
J (JULIET)	MAX FLT LVL TEMP--The maximum temperature observed within 5 nm of the center fix coordinates. If a higher temperature is observed at a location more than 5 nm away from the flight level center (item BRAVO), it is reported in Remarks, including bearing and distance from the flight level center. PRESSURE ALT--Pressure altitude data (meters) are taken at the same location as the maximum temperature data reported in item JULIET.
K (KILO)	Dewpoint temperature/sea surface temperatures are collected at the same location as the maximum temperature reported in item JULIET. Enter NA if not observed.
L (LIMA)	Only report if at least 50 percent of the center has an eyewall, otherwise enter NA. Closed wall--if the center has 100 percent coverage with no eyewall weakness. Open XX--if the center has 50 percent or more but less than 100 percent coverage. State the direction of the eyewall weakness. Spiral band--report Item Juliet with the best approximation of the shape/diameter of the inner core.
M (MIKE)	Self-explanatory. Report only if item LIMA is reported, otherwise enter NA.
N (NOVEMBER)	Fix determined by: Always report 1. Report 2 if radar indicates curvature or banding consistent with fix location. Report 3 if recorded or observed winds indicate a closed center. Report 4 if the fix pressure is lower than all reported on the inbound leg. Report 5 if the fix temperature is at least higher than any reported on the inbound leg. Fix level: Report 0 alone if fix is made solely on surface winds. Report 0 and the flight-level code if the centers are within 5 nm of each other.
O (OSCAR)	Navigational and meteorological accuracy are reported as the upper limit of probable error. Meteorological accuracy is normally reported as one-half of the diameter of the light and variable wind center.
P (PAPA)	Remarks to enhance the data reported above. Required remarks include: (1) mission identifier and observation number; (2) the maximum flight level wind observed, time of observation, and the bearing and range from the flight level center of the observed wind on the latest pass through any octant of the storm, i.e., 337.5-22.5 degrees, 22.5-67.5 degrees, etc.; (3) the maximum flight-level wind observed on the outbound leg following the center fix just obtained, if it is higher than the inbound maximum reported in item F. Include time of observation and the bearing and range from the flight level center of the qualifying outbound max wind. If, after the transmission of the vortex message but prior to the aircraft reaching the cross-leg turn point, a higher qualifying outbound wind is observed, then the vortex message will be amended with the higher outbound wind reported. If the outbound max FL wind becomes the new overall max FL wind, then consolidate the two max FL wind remarks into one remark: MAX FL WIND 73 KT 081 / 25 NM 23:30:30Z MAX OUTBOUND FL WIND 55 KT 083 / 14 NM 01:36:00Z MAX OUTBOUND AND MAX FL WIND 55 KT 083 / 14 NM 01:36:00Z

	(4) surface wind direction and speed from the center dropsonde, if available: CNTR DROPSONDE SFC WIND 265 / 12 KT (5) the method of deriving the central SLP when extrapolated; and (6) the bearing and range of the surface center and/or maximum flight level temperature if not within 5 nm of the flight level center.

```
URNT12 KNHC 072030
VORTEX DATA MESSAGE AL092008
A. 07/20:09:20Z
B. 21 deg 01 min N
   074 deg 26 min W
C. 700 mb 2624 m
D. 90 kt
E. 045 deg 13 nm
F. 147 deg 106 kt
G. 047 deg 016 nm
H. 945 mb
I. 10 C/ 3045 m
J. 16 C/ 3057 m
K. 13 C/ NA
L. CLOSED WALL
M. CO16-48
N. 12345/7
O. 0.02 / 1 nm
P. AF307 0909A IKE        OB 11
MAX FL WIND 107 KT 135 / 20 NM 18:21:10Z
```

Figure 5-4. Example Vortex Data Message (VDM) for the WC-130J

NHOP COORDINATED REQUEST FOR AIRCRAFT RECONNAISSANCE

___ Original

___ Amendment

(Check One)

I. ATLANTIC REQUIREMENTS

STORM NAME DEPRESSION # SUSPECT AREA	FIX OR ON STATION TIME	COORDINATES	FLIGHT PATTERN	FCST MVMT	NHC PRIORITY

GULF STREAM _____

SUCCEEDING DAY OUTLOOK _____

REMARKS _____

II. PACIFIC REQUIREMENTS

STORM NAME DEPRESSION # SUSPECT AREA	FIX OR ON STATION TIME	COORDINATES	FLIGHT PATTERN	FCST MVMT	NHC PRIORITY

SUCCEEDING DAY OUTLOOK _____

REMARKS _____

III. DISTRIBUTION

A. TO CARCAH BY 1630Z OR AMEND AT ANY TIME

B. Date _____ Time _____ FCSTR INITIAL _____

C. 53 WRS _____ AOC _____ Other _____

Figure 5-5. NHOP Coordinated Request for Aircraft Reconnaissance

```
┌─────────────────────────────────────────────────────────────────────────┐
│                  TROPICAL CYCLONE PLAN OF THE DAY FORMAT                   │
│                   ATLANTIC AND CENTRAL PACIFIC OCEANS                      │
│                                                                           │
│  NOUS42 KNHC _____ (DATE/UTC TIME)                                    │
│  WEATHER RECONNAISSANCE FLIGHTS                                           │
│  CARCAH, NATIONAL HURRICANE CENTER, MIAMI, FL                             │
│  _____ (LOCAL TIME) ___ (TIME ZONE) ___ (DAY) ___ (MONTH/DATE), ____ (YEAR)│
│  SUBJECT: THE TROPICAL CYCLONE PLAN OF THE DAY (TCPOD)                    │
│  VALID _____Z (MONTH) TO _____Z (MONTH) (YEAR)                          │
│  TCPOD NUMBER.........(YR)- _____                                     │
│  I.    ATLANTIC REQUIREMENTS                                              │
│     1.   (STORM NAME, DEPRESSION, SUSPECT AREA) or (NEGATIVE RECON RQMTS) │
│          FLIGHT ONE (NHC PRIORITY, if applicable)                        │
│             TEAL or NOAA _____ (number)                                   │
│                A. _____Z    FIX/INVEST TIME        │
│                B. _____     MISSION IDENTIFIER      │
│                C. _____Z    DEPARTURE TIME          │
│                D. _____     FORECAST POSITION       │
│                E. _____Z    TIME ON STATION         │
│                F. _____     ALTITUDE(S) ON STATION  │
│                G. _____     REMARKS (if needed)     │
│          FLIGHT TWO (if applicable, same as FLIGHT ONE)                   │
│     2.   (SECOND SYSTEM, if applicable, same as in 1. above)             │
│     3.   OUTLOOK FOR SUCCEEDING DAY (NHC PRIORITY, if applicable)        │
│                A.  POSSIBLE  (Unit)  ON STATION REQUIREMENT NEAR (Location) AT │
│                    (Time) Z.                                              │
│  II.   PACIFIC REQUIREMENTS (Same as in ATLANTIC)                        │
└─────────────────────────────────────────────────────────────────────────┘
```

Figure 5-6. Tropical Cyclone Plan of the Day Format

5.5.1.3. **Anticipated Reconnaissance Requests.** Reconnaissance requests can be anticipated for a forecast or actual storm location.

5.5.1.3.1. For the Atlantic, Gulf of Mexico, Caribbean, and Central Pacific areas, the requests can be:
- Up to four 6-hourly fixes per day when a storm is within 500 nm of landfall and west of 52.5°W in the Atlantic.
- Up to eight 3-hourly fixes per day when a storm is forecast to be within 300 nm of the U.S. coast, Hawaiian Islands, Puerto Rico, Virgin Islands, DOD installations, and other DOD assets when specified.
- Up to two synoptic surveillance missions per 24-hour period for potentially land-falling storms.

5.5.1.3.2. In the Eastern Pacific, reconnaissance missions may be tasked when necessary to carry out warning responsibilities.

5.5.1.3.3. Investigative flights may be requested for disturbances in areas defined above, i.e., one or two flights per day dependent upon proximity of landfall and upon known or suspected stage of development.

5.5.1.3.4. Exceptions may be made when additional reconnaissance is essential to carry out warning responsibilities.

5.5.2. **DOD and DOC Reconnaissance Aircraft Responsiveness.**

5.5.2.1. **Requirement Notification.** Notification of requirements must proceed tasked-on-station time by at least 16 hours plus en route time to the area of concern.

5.5.2.2. **Prepositioning.** The "Succeeding Day Outlook" portion of the TCPOD provides advance notification of requirements and authorizes units to preposition aircraft to forward operating locations. For missions requiring prepositioning, the "Succeeding Day Outlook" may not provide adequate advance notification. In this situation, an "Additional Day Outlook" may be included in the TCPOD to authorize units to preposition aircraft.

5.5.2.3. **Resources Permitting.** When circumstances preclude the appropriate notification lead time, the requirement will be levied as "resources permitting." When a "resources permitting" requirement is levied in an amendment, the NHC will indicate the priority of all existing or remaining requirements.

5.5.2.4. **Emergency Requirement.** If a storm develops unexpectedly and could cause a serious threat to lives and property within a shorter time than provided for in the paragraphs above, CARCAH will contact the reconnaissance units, or higher headquarters, as appropriate, and request assistance in implementing emergency procedures not covered in this plan. The NHC and CPHC directors have authority to declare an emergency.

5.5.2.5.   NOAA WP-3D Availability. At least one WP-3D will be operationally configured (per paragraph 5.4.7) and available to respond to requirements within 24-hours from June 1 through November 30 annually. A second WP-3D with the same operational configuration will be available each hurricane season from July 15 to September 30. When maintenance and programmatic considerations permit, the second aircraft could be made available until November 30 also. The frequency of flights when two aircraft are available and with present staffing shall be every 12 hours.

5.5.3.   Reconnaissance Tropical Cyclone Plan of the Day.

5.5.3.1.   Preparation. CARCAH will coordinate the TCPOD (Figure 5-6) daily during the period from June 1 to November 30 and at other times during the year as required. Transmitted TCPODs will be serially numbered each season.

5.5.3.1.1. CARCAH will coordinate the TCPOD with NHC, the 53 WRS, and NOAA AOC before publication.

5.5.3.1.1.1. The coordinated TCPOD is the agency's RFA to DOD. Since DOD's support to NOAA is congressionally mandated and funded through the DOD Appropriations Act, the coordinated TCPOD is considered a validated and approved RFA.

5.5.3.1.1.2. Combatant command headquarters and their air component command headquarters will coordinate on missions by reviewing the proposed TCPOD posted at http://www.nhc.noaa.gov/reconlist.shtml, then click 'For Tomorrow' under 'Plan of the Day.'

5.5.3.1.1.3. Combatant command headquarters and their air component command headquarters will pull current DOD missions from http://www.nhc.noaa.gov/reconlist.shtml, then click 'For Today' under 'Plan of the Day.' Additionally, the 403rd Current Operations provides a mission setup sheet with reason of deviation from TCPOD, as required, to the combatant command and their air component operations/command centers.

5.5.3.1.2. The TCPOD will list all DOC/NOAA AOC and DOD required tropical and subtropical cyclone operational reconnaissance missions. Research missions will also be listed in the TCPOD when available by transmission time.

5.5.3.1.3. Amendments to the TCPOD will be published only when requirements change. When amended, the impact on each listed flight will be identified (i.e., No Change, Change Added, or Cancel).

5.5.3.2.   Dissemination. The TCPOD will be made available to appropriate agencies, such as FAA, DOD, and NOAA, which provide support to or control of reconnaissance aircraft or are a part of the tropical cyclone warning service. Under normal circumstances, the TCPOD will be disseminated by 1830 UTC each day including weekends and holidays. If there are no current day or succeeding-day reconnaissance requirements, a negative report, which covers the appropriate time frame, will be disseminated. Amendments will be disseminated as required.

[NOTE: The TCPOD is disseminated under the header "MIAREPRPD" for AWIPS users and "NOUS42 KNHC" for AWDS users. The TCPOD can be accessed via the Internet at the National Hurricane Center homepage at www.nhc.noaa.gov, then click on 'Aircraft Reconnaissance' and then on 'Plan of the Day.']

5.6. Reconnaissance Effectiveness Criteria.

5.6.1. **General.** Specified reconnaissance times are established to allow sufficient time for the forecaster to analyze the data before issuing an advisory. Every effort should be made to obtain data at scheduled times. The following criteria will be used to assess reconnaissance mission effectiveness:

5.6.1.1. **Tropical Cyclone Fix Mission.**
- ONTIME. The fix is made no earlier than 1 hour before nor later than ½ hour after scheduled fix time.
- EARLY. The fix is made from 1 hour before scheduled fix time to one-half of the time interval to the preceding scheduled fix, not to exceed 3 hours.
- LATE. The fix is made within the interval from ½ hour after scheduled fix time to one-half of the time interval to the succeeding scheduled fix, not to exceed 3 hours.
- MISSED. Data are not obtained within the parameters specified for on-time, early, or late.

[NOTE: Appropriate credit will be given when the aircraft arrives in the requested area but is unable to locate a center due to storm dissipation, the absence of a fixable center, or rapid movement. Credit will also be given for radar fixes if penetration is not possible due to geographic or other flight restrictions.]

5.6.1.2. **Tropical Cyclone Investigative Missions.**
- ONTIME. An observation must be taken within 250 nm of the specified coordinates by the scheduled time.
- LATE. An observation is taken within 250 nm of the specified coordinates after the scheduled time but not later than the scheduled time plus 2 hours.
- MISSED. When the aircraft fails to be within the 250 nm of the specific coordinates by the scheduled time plus 2 hours or is unable to provide meaningful data.

5.6.1.3. Synoptic Surveillance Missions.

- SATISFIED. Requirements are considered satisfied upon completion of the assigned track and the acquired dropwindsonde data are transmitted from the aircraft prior to the WPC/OPC deadline for synoptic analysis.
- MISSED. When the requirements listed above are not satisfied.

5.6.2. Mission Assessment. The NHC or CPHC will provide CARCAH a written assessment of the reconnaissance mission anytime its timeliness or quality is outstanding or substandard (see Figure 5-7). Mission requirements levied as "resources permitting" will not be assessed for timeliness but may be assessed for quality of data gathered.

5.6.3. Summaries. CARCAH will maintain monthly and seasonal reconnaissance summaries, detailing requirements tasked by NHC and CPHC and missions accomplished.

5.7. Aerial Reconnaissance Weather Encoding, Reporting, and Coordination.

5.7.1. Vortex Data. A vortex data message (Figure 5-4) will be prepared for all fixes, using all observed vortex fix information, each time the aircraft penetrates the center. The inner core radar reflectivity imagery would be provided at a rate of one image per Vortex Data Message and be sent within 30 minutes of transmission of the Vortex Data Message.

5.7.2. Aircraft Radar Fix Data. When proximity to land, air traffic control restriction, or other factors prevent actual penetration of the vortex by the reconnaissance aircraft, it is permissible to fix the cyclone by radar. Radar fixes may be reported in a vortex data message using available observed information or as a remark appended to a RECCO observation taken at fix time. The remark stating the type of radar fix and quality of the radar presentation is in accordance with chapter 8, paragraph 8.3.2. Two examples follow:

Example 1: RADAR FIX PSBL CENTER 21.5N 83.0W, POOR RADAR PRESENTATION, SPIRAL BAND, MET ACCURACY 15NM

Example 2: RADAR FIX EYE 21 DEG 23 MIN N 78 DEG 42 MIN W GOOD RADAR PRESENTATION CIRCULAR EYE DIAM 25 NM OPEN SW.

5.7.3. Peripheral Data. Storm penetration and collection of peripheral data will normally begin at the operational altitude approximately 105 nm from the center as determined by the flight meteorologist.

5.7.4. Mission Coordination. Mission coordination for all missions will be accomplished through CARCAH. Meteorological discussions for Central Pacific missions may be accomplished directly with the CPHC; however, any changes to tasking will be accomplished through CARCAH.

5.7.5. Post-flight Debriefing. Unless otherwise directed, the flight meteorologist will provide either an airborne or post-flight debriefing to the appropriate hurricane center through CARCAH to ensure all observations were received and understood.

5.7.6. Mission Identifier. Regular weather and hurricane reconnaissance messages will include the five-digit agency/aircraft indicator followed by the CARCAH-assigned mission/storm-system indicator. Table 5-3 summarizes elements of the mission identifier.

5.7.7. Storm Identifier <Storm ID>. To facilitate the automatic ingest into the NHC, CPHC, and DOD tropical cyclone forecast computing systems, the storm identifier will be added 3 spaces after the Vortex Data Message title (see Figure 5-4) in the following format: **Vortex Data Message BBCCYYYY.** For the definition of BBCCYYYY, see Chapter 4, paragraph 4.3.3.

5.7.8. Observation Numbering and Content. Air Force aircraft movement information (i.e., departure time and location, and ETA's to locations) will not be included in observation remarks. That information should be passed to CARCAH via SATCOM administrative messages. The mission identifier will be the first mandatory remark followed by the observation number. All observations (RECCO, vortex, dropsonde) from the first to the last will be numbered sequentially. HDOBs will be automatically numbered sequentially but separately from other observations. When an aircraft is diverted from its original mission to fulfill NHC requirements, conclude the original mission by using the last report remark.

The next observation from the diverted aircraft will use the CARCAH-assigned mission identifier, will be numbered OB 01, and will include the time of diversion.

EXAMPLE

RMK AF306 0lBBA INVEST OB 01 DPTD AF306 WXWXA AT 05/1235Z

MISSION EVALUATION FORM

MEMORANDUM FOR: OL-A, 53 WRS/CARCAH

FROM:_____(Director, NHC, CPHC)_____ _____

SUBJECT: Mission _____Evaluation
                              (Mission Identifier)

PUBLISHED REQUIREMENTS:

  Premission Coordinates (As Updated Prior to TKO)_____N_____W

  Flight Pattern _____

  Mission Requirements Times _____

RECONNAISSANCE MISSION PERFORMANCE:

  Flight Flown: _____Completely   _____Partially   _____Other

  Horizontal Data Coverage: _____Complete   _____Timely   _____Accurate
                             _____Incomplete   _____Untimely   _____Inaccurate

  Vertical Data Coverage: _____Complete   _____Timely   _____Accurate
                             _____Incomplete   _____Untimely   _____Inaccurate

  Requirements Accomplished: _____On Time   _____Early   _____Late
                             _____Missed

OVERALL MISSION EVALUATION:

   OUTSTANDING_____

   UNSATISFACTORY_____   FOR:

    COMPLETENESS_____   TIMELINESS_____   ACCURACY_____

    EQUIPMENT_____   PROCEDURES_____   OTHER_____

REMARKS: (Brief but specific)

_____
FORECASTER's SIGNATURE

Figure 5-7. Mission Evaluation Form

Table 5-3. Elements of the Mission Identifier

AGENCY/ AIRCRAFT	Mission Storm System Indicator			
Agency + Aircraft Number[12]	Sequential number of mission in this storm	Two-digit depression number or two letter identifier if not a depression or greater[3]	Location A, E, C, or W[4]	Storm name or mission type (i.e., CYCLONE or INVEST
EXAMPLES				
AF306 0201C CYCLONE	USAF aircraft 5306 on the second mission for Tropical or Subtropical Depression One in the Central Pacific. Mission type can be fix or surveillance, as specified in the TCPOD.			
AF307 0403E CARLOS	USAF aircraft 5307 on the fourth mission for the third classified tropical or subtropical system that formed in the Eastern Pacific and acquired the name Carlos.			
NOAA2 01BBA INVEST	NOAA aircraft 42RF on the first mission to investigate the second unclassified suspect area in the Atlantic, Gulf of Mexico, or Caribbean.			
NOAA9 WAWXA AL92	NOAA aircraft N49RF on the first flight of a sequence of non-tasked research missions into Atlantic suspect area AL92.			
NOAA3 WF13A KARL	NOAA aircraft N43RF on the sixth flight of a sequence of non-tasked research missions into the system that developed from suspect area AL92 into the thirteenth tropical or subtropical cyclone in the Atlantic Basin and acquired the name Karl.			

5.7.9   Corrections to Observations. A correction indicator should be appended to the WMO abbreviated header after the date/time group and to any lines containing the mission identifier and observation number within corrected aircraft messages. This includes the first remark line in a RECCO, Item P in a vortex data, each of the 61616 lines in a sonde TEMP DROP code, and the second line in an HDOB data message. The first corrected message will have an indicator of CCA; subsequent corrections will have indicators of CCB, CCC, etc. Examples of corrected observations are in Table 5-4 below:

---

[1] AF plus last 3 digits of tail number
[2] NOAA, plus last digit of aircraft registration number
[3] The letters CC should not be used in an invest identifier
[4] A=Atlantic, Caribbean, or Gulf of Mexico; E=Eastern Pacific; C=Central Pacific; W=Western Pacific

Table 5-4. Examples of Corrected Observations

EXAMPLES	
URNT11 KNHC 111629 CCA 97779 16264 51286 90000 30400 09054 11071 /3136 40545 RMK AF303 2709A IKE OB 01 CCA	Correction for RECCO message OB 01 from the AF303 02709A IKE mission.
URNT12 KNHC 130552 CCB VORTEX DATA MESSAGE AL092008 A. 13/04:47:20Z B. 28 deg 52 min N 094 deg 37 min W . . . P. AF301 3509A IKE OB 02 CCB MAX FL WIND 103 KT 135 / 20 NM 04:30:40Z CORRECTED FOR TIME IN ITEM A	Second correction for vortex data message OB 02 from the AF301 3509A IKE mission.
UZNT13 KWBC 080739 CCA XXAA 58062 99300 70760 11606 99/// ///// ///// 00956 25616 09512 . . . 61616 NOAA9 1109A IKE OB 03 CCA 62626 0629 LST WND 894 AEV 20704 CORRECTED RPT DLM WND 08509 0071 82 = XXBB 58068 99300 70760 11606 00/// ///// 11007 26217 22977 24010 . . . 61616 NOAA9 1109A IKE OB 03 CCA 62626 0629 LST WND 894 AEV 20704 CORRECTED RPT DLM WND 08509 0071 82 =	Correction for sonde TEMP DROP code message OB 03 from the NOAA9 1109A IKE mission.

5.8. **Operational Flight Patterns.** This section details the operational flight patterns that provide vortex and peripheral data on tropical and subtropical cyclones.

5.8.1. Flight Pattern ALPHA Operational Details.

5.8.1.1. **Flight Levels and Sequence.** Flight levels will normally be 1,500 ft, 925 hPa, 850 hPa, or 700 hPa, depending on data requirements and flight safety. Legs will normally be 105 nm long and flown on intercardinal tracks (45 degrees off cardinal tracks). The flight sequence is shown in Figure 5-8. The pattern can be started at any intercardinal point and then repeated throughout the mission. Prior to starting an inbound or outbound track the aircrew should evaluate all available data, e.g., radar presentation, satellite photo, for flight safety. Once started on course, every effort should be made to maintain a straight track and the tasked altitude. A horizontal observation is required at each leg end point. This data is transmitted immediately.

The ALPHA pattern may be modified to satisfy unique customer requirements (such as extending legs to examine the wind profile of a strong storm) or because of proximity of land or warning areas.

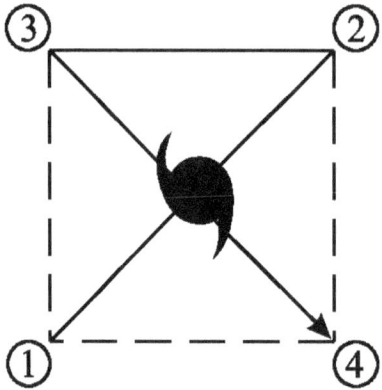

Figure 5-8. Flight Pattern ALPHA

5.8.1.2.   Vortex fix data. On each transit of the center a fix will be made and a vortex data message completed, using data gathered on the inbound track since the previous fix and will be transmitted immediately. Center dropsonde data will also be provided for scheduled fixes made at 850 hPa or above. The dropsonde will be released at the flight-level center coordinates (item BRAVO of the vortex data message). For fixes when dropsonde-measured SLP is not available, an extrapolated SLP will be computed and reported.

5.8.2. Investigative Missions. An investigative mission is tasked on tropical or subtropical disturbances to determine the existence or non-existence of a closed circulation, supply reconnaissance observations in required areas, and locate the vortex center, if any.

5.8.2.1.   Flight Levels. Flight level will normally be at or below 1,500 ft absolute altitude but may be adjusted as dictated by data requirements, meteorological conditions, or flying safety factors.

5.8.2.2.   Vortex Fix. A vortex data message is required if a vortex fix is made.

5.8.2.3.   Closed Circulation. A closed circulation is supported by at least one sustained wind reported in each quadrant of the cyclone. Surface winds are preferred.

5.8.2.4.   Flight Pattern. The preferred approach is to fly to the tasked coordinates of the forecasted center and then execute a pattern as observed conditions dictate. Suggested patterns are the X, Box, or Delta patterns, but the flight meteorologist may choose any approach. See Figure 5-9. Turns are usually made to take advantage of tailwinds whenever possible. Note: The depicted pattern may be converted to a mirror image if entry is made from a different direction.

-   On the X pattern, the aircraft is turned to head directly towards the center, as indicated by the surface or flight level winds. The aircraft is flown through the calm center until winds from the opposite direction occur (second quadrant). The aircraft is then turned to a cardinal heading until a wind shift occurs (third quadrant). Finally, the aircraft is turned towards the center and flown straight through the center to the last quadrant.

- On the Box pattern, the aircraft is flown on cardinal headings around the suspected center. The track resembles three sides of a square.
- On the Delta pattern, the aircraft is flown on a cardinal heading to pass 60 nm from the forecasted center. After observing a wind shift (second quadrant) the aircraft is turned to pass through the center until winds from the opposite direction occur (third quadrant). Finally, the aircraft is turned on a cardinal heading (parallel to the initial heading) to pick up the fourth quadrant winds. If data indicate that the aircraft is far north of any existing circulation, the pattern is extended as shown by the dashed lines.

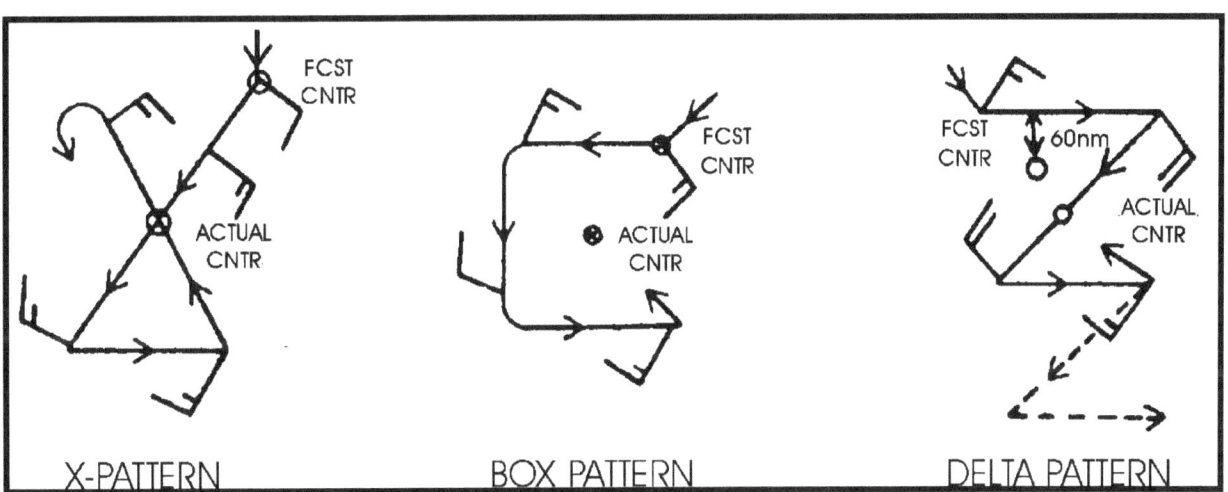

Figure 5-9. Suggested Patterns for Investigative Missions

5.8.3. Synoptic Surveillance Missions. A synoptic surveillance mission is tasked to measure the large-scale wind and thermodynamic fields within approximately 800 nautical miles of tropical cyclones. Specific flight tracks will vary depending on storm location and synoptic situation, and multiple aircraft may be required to satisfy surveillance mission requirements.

5.8.4. Eyewall and Outer-Wind Field Sampling Modules. These are patterns of dropwindsonde releases designed to measure the maximum surface wind, as well as the extent of hurricane and tropical storm force surface winds. They are meant to be flown using the operational alpha pattern. Dropwindsonde releases in these modules are in addition to any other releases required by Table 5-1.

5.8.4.1.   Eyewall Module. While executing a standard alpha pattern to satisfy a fix requirement, one sounding will be taken during each inbound and outbound passage through the eyewall (except as noted below), for a total of four soundings. The releases should be made at or just inward (within 12 km) of the flight-level radius of maximum wind (RMW). If the radar presentation is suitable, the inner edge of the radar eyewall may be used to identify the release point. If possible, and when resources and safety permit, two dropwindsondes, spaced less than 30 seconds apart, should be deployed on the inbound leg on the side of the storm believed to have the highest surface winds (normally the right-hand side). In this case, the outer of the two releases should be made at the RMW, with the second release following as soon as possible. Typically, the eyewall module will be tasked within 48 hours of a forecasted hurricane landfall.

5.8.4.2.   Outer-Wind Field Module. On an alpha pattern, deploy dropwindsondes at 50 nm intervals from the center on each of two successive inbound and outbound legs, outward to 200 nm. A release should also be made at the midpoint of the cross (downwind) leg, for a total of 19 soundings, including center drops. The length of the legs and the sounding interval may be adjusted, depending on the size of the storm.

5.9.   Aircraft Reconnaissance Communications.

5.9.1.   General. The 53 WRS WC-130 aircraft will normally transmit reconnaissance observations via the Air Force Satellite Communications System (AFSATCOM) or commercial SATCOM. Figures 5-10 and 5-11 depict the NOAA and AFSATCOM communications links. The NOAA G-IV and WP-3D will normally transmit WMO Temp Drop messages via commercial SATCOM. Flight meteorologists should contact CARCAH following the first fix, and periodically throughout the mission.

5.9.2.   Backup Air-to-Ground Communications. The weather reconnaissance crew may relay weather data via SATPHONE or HF phone patch to the weather data monitor. Monitors will evaluate these reports and disseminate them through the Air Force's Automated Weather Network (AWN) or to the weather communications facility at Suitland, Maryland. Specific radio procedures and terminology will comply with Allied Communications Publication 125, Standard Telephone and Radio Procedures.

5.9.3.   Aircraft-to-Satellite Data Link (ASDL)-Equipped Aircraft. Aircraft equipped with ASDL have the option to utilize the ASDL system. Prior to the beginning of the hurricane season, each ASDL-equipped aircraft will perform a ground or airborne test of the equipment and data ground handling procedures to determine the equipment reliability, transmission errors, and time lapse between transmission of the data from the aircraft and receipt of the data by the hurricane forecaster. Test data will be forwarded to the Chair, Working Group for Hurricane and Winter Storms Operations and Research.

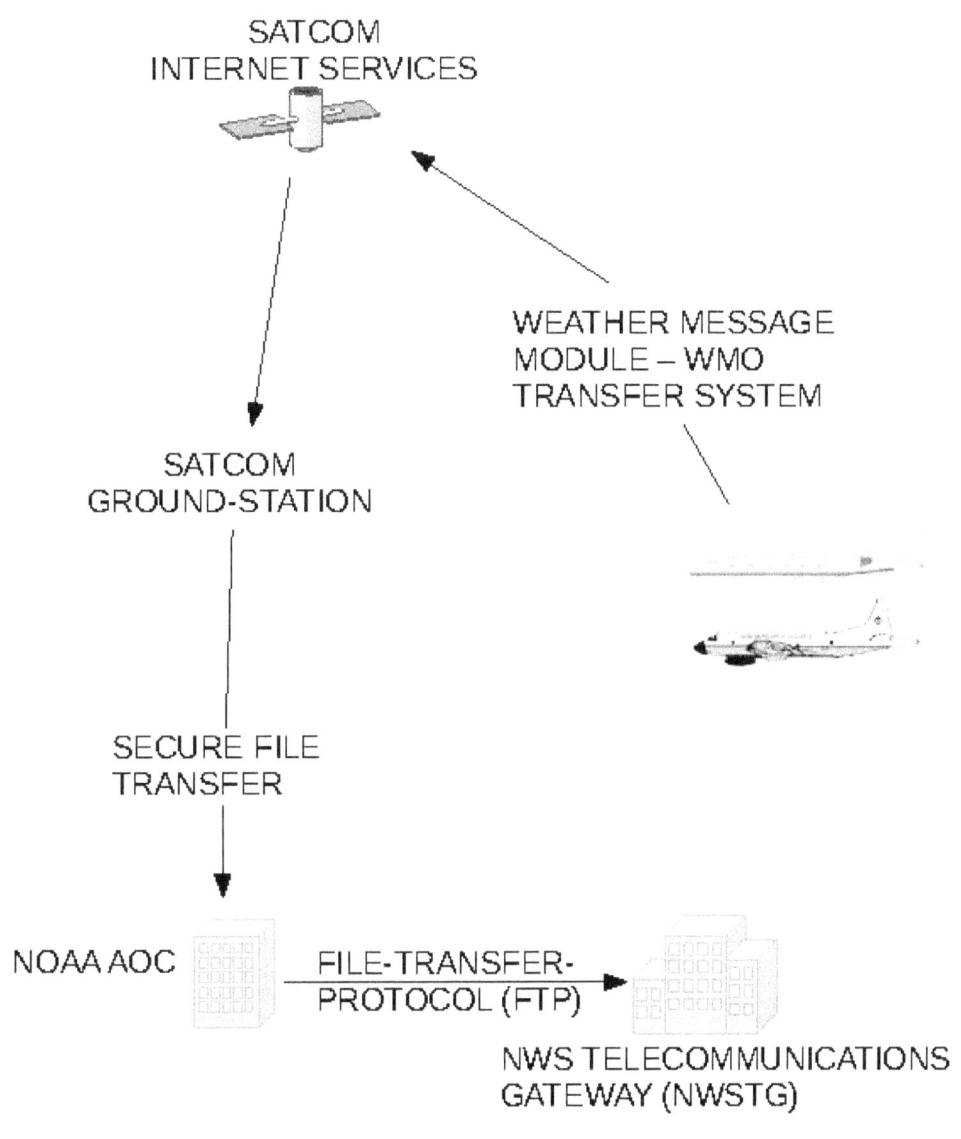

Figure 5-10. Schematic of WMO Message Path for NOAA G-IV and P-3Aircraft

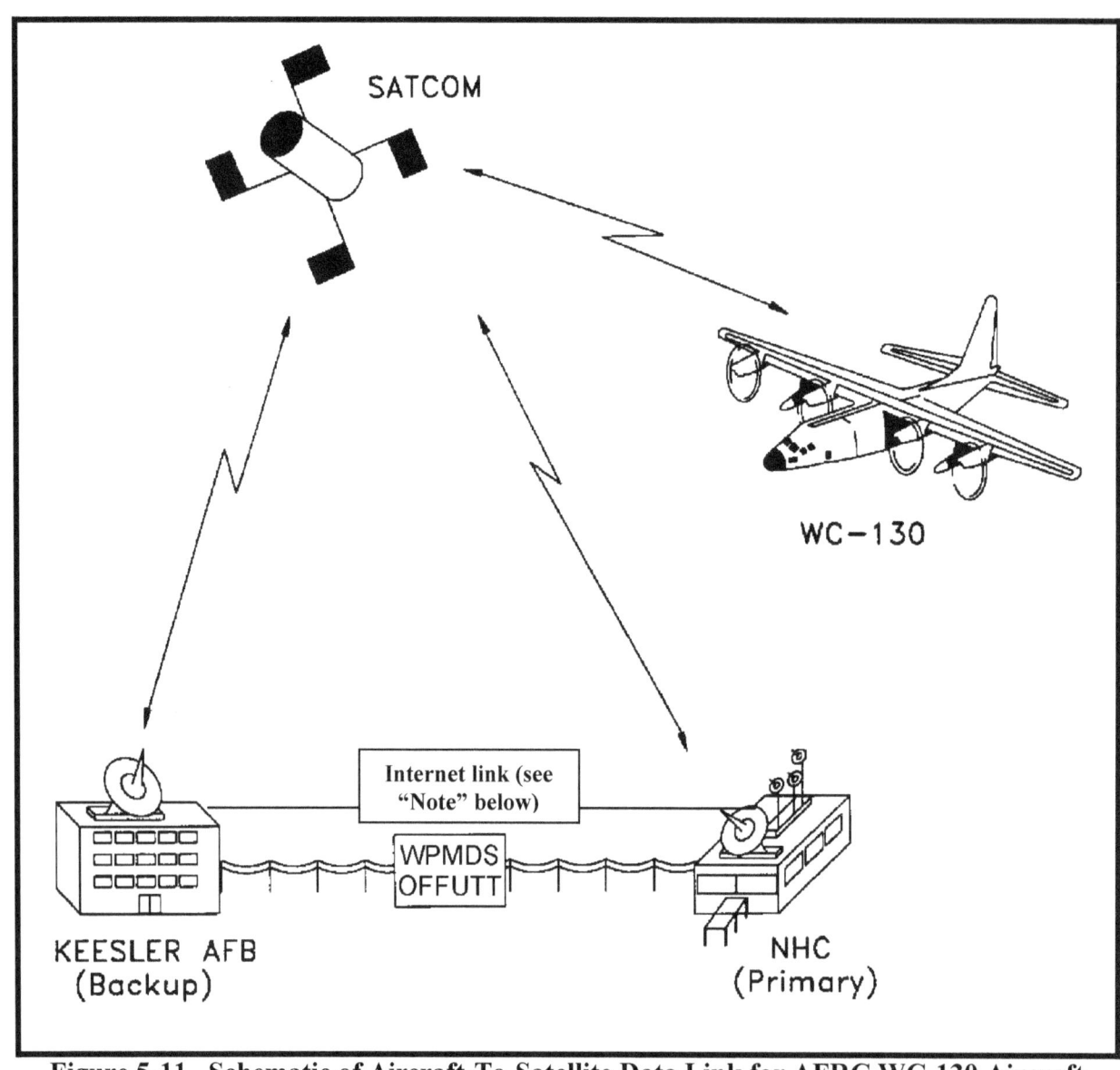

Figure 5-11. Schematic of Aircraft-To-Satellite Data Link for AFRC WC-130 Aircraft

[Note: An Internet link from Keesler AFB to NHC provides the capability for all observation types to be passed directly to NHC without going through Offutt Air Force Base.]

5.9.4. Backup CARCAH Procedures. Satellite ground stations, which are used to receive and process data from AFRC reconnaissance aircraft, are installed at CARCAH (located within NHC) and the 53 WRS (located at Keesler Air Force Base). The 53 WRS ground station has a similar configuration and communications capability as the satellite ground station installed a CARCAH, except that the CARCAH ground station has additional capability to stream data using serial RS-232 communications to NHC local servers. The ground station at the 53 WRS can fully transmit data using SATCOM and land line to the CARCAH ground station. Both ground stations can send data to AFWA's Weather Product Management and Distribution System (WPMDS)—WPMDS then relays all AFRC/53 WRS reconnaissance data to the NWS Gateway for world-wide distribution. In the event that backup procedures are required due to severe communications failures, severe weather conditions, or other extreme events affecting NHC, some or all CARCAH responsibilities will be transferred to the 53 WRS, ensuring reconnaissance service is uninterrupted.

5.9.4.1. Satellite Antenna Communications Failure at NHC. If an outage is expected to be temporary, CARCAH will coordinate with the 53 WRS to have operators man the ground station located at the backup site. They will be responsible for maintaining contact with airborne reconnaissance aircraft and relaying data via land line to the CARCAH ground station. In the event communications lines between the backup site and NHC are also severed, the 53 WRS ground station will be configured to transmit data directly to the WPMDS. No procedure is currently implemented for sending the aircraft data directly to local servers at WPC or CPHC (NHC's COOP backup site); consequently, all data or observations will need to be accessed from the WPMDS or obtained from the NWS Gateway.

For long-term outages, CARCAH will send personnel to the backup site. They will monitor the aircraft data and ensure they are transmitted to the WPMDS, NWS servers, and external users from that location.

5.9.4.2. Internet Communications Failure. In the event there is a long-term network communications outage between NHC and AFWA, the CARCAH ground station will still be able to receive aircraft data and send them to local NHC servers. If Internet access problems originate at NHC, the CARCAH ground station will be configured to relay the data to the backup site ground station via SATCOM. The 53 WRS ground station will in turn be configured to automatically transmit them to the AFWA WPMDS server. However, if the Internet disruptions occur at AFWA, no data can be sent to the AWN, NWS servers, and external users until service is restored.

5.9.4.3. NHC Emergency Backup Plan. In the event NHC activates the WPC or CPHC COOP backup plan, designated CARCAH personnel will deploy to the backup site to operate the 53 WRS ground station. The reconnaissance data will be obtained at the WPC COOP site either through the WPMDS or the NWS Gateway.

CHAPTER 6

AIRSPACE OPERATIONS

6.1. Pre-mission Coordination.

6.1.1. Federal Aviation Administration (FAA) Coordination.

6.1.1.1. Responsibilities. The Air Traffic Control System Command Center (ATCSCC) and Air Route Traffic Control Centers (ARTCC) are responsible for coordination in support of the NHOP.

6.1.1.2. ATCSCC Procedures.

- Review the TCPOD available at http://www.nhc.noaa.gov/reconlist.shtml, by 1830 UTC. Normal notification of scheduled NHOP flights is accomplished through the TCPOD (1 June through 30 November).
- Activate the Hurricane Desk, when required.
- Review the Mission Coordination Sheet (see Appendix L). Prepare a public Flow Evaluation Area (FEA) based on the latitude/longitude points specified in the Mission Coordination sheet when a mission is scheduled to be flown. The FEA naming convention is the aircraft call sign. Modify the FEA when requested by the affected facilities. (The flying unit will fax their Mission Coordination Sheet to the ATCSCC and affected ARTCCs 1-2 hours prior to flight departure time).
- Coordinate with the impacted ARTCCs as required and designate a Primary ARTCC when the Operations Area includes multiple ARTCCs.
- In the event of an unscheduled mission that is not listed on the TCPOD, the flying unit will contact the ATCSCC. The ATCSCC will initiate a conference call with the unit and all affected ARTCCs.
- When requested, assist ARTCCs with traffic flow priorities if the hurricane reconnaissance flight will impact air traffic. The hurricane reconnaissance flight receives priority as specified in JO Order 7110.65.
- Coordinate with Air Traffic Services Cell (ATSC), as needed, when informed by an ARTCC of a disapproval of hurricane reconnaissance flight to enter a Special Use Airspace (SUA) or Special Activity Airspace (SAA).
- Conduct hurricane and customer teleconferences, as necessary.

6.1.1.3. ARTCC Procedures.

- Review the TCPOD at http://www.nhc.noaa.gov/reconlist.shtml, by 1830 UTC. Normal notification of scheduled NHOP flights is accomplished through the TCPOD (1 June through 30 November).
- Review the Mission Coordination Sheet (see Appendix L) - the flying unit will fax their Mission Coordination Sheet to the ATCSCC and affected ARTCCs 1-2 hours prior to flight departure time.
- Coordinate with all impacted Center and Terminal facilities within their area of responsibility.

- Coordinate with all impacted military facilities (e.g., FACSFAC) through the applicable Military Operation Desks within their area of operations and responsibility to ensure all offshore airspace (i.e., Warning Areas, SUA, SAA) that is activated by the military is protected for NHOP flights, when required. If SUA or SAA release is not approved, contact the ATCSCC.
- When requested, assign 53 WRS and NOAA aircraft the dedicated NORAD transponder code associated with their call sign, which is listed on the Mission Coordination Sheet.
- When designated by ATCSCC as the Primary ARTCC, responsibilities will include:
  - Coordinate with CARCAH and aircrew(s) on flight plan specifics, when necessary.
  - If the mission profile changes, coordinate with the ATCSCC for FEA modifications, and ensure affected ARTCCs are aware of the change.
  - Advise the ATCSCC and affected ARTCCs of any mission cancellation or delay information received from the flying unit.

6.1.2. Pre-Mission Coordination.

6.1.2.1. Flying Agencies (other than the 53 WRS or NOAA AOC) Pre-mission Coordination.

- NASA, NRL, NSF or any other agency planning research missions, including Unmanned Aircraft Systems (UAS), into or around the forecast or actual storm location will coordinate with affected ARTCCs and CARCAH as soon as possible prior to all flights.
- The flying unit will fax their Mission Coordination Sheet to the ATCSCC and affected ARTCCs 1-2 hours prior to flight departure time.
- Flights in support of the NHOP (conducted by the 53 WRS and NOAA AOC operations) are normally published in the TCPOD at http://www.nhc.noaa.gov/reconlist.shtml by 1830 UTC. Reference the TCPOD to assist in de-confliction efforts. Required operational reconnaissance missions flown by the 53 WRS and NOAA AOC will be outlined in the TCPOD. Flights other than 53 WRS and NOAA AOC tasked operational missions should be listed in the TCPOD remarks section.
- CARCAH coordination is normally restricted to what is required between the 53 WRS, NOAA AOC, NHC, and ARTCCs in support of operational tasking. Due to staffing constraints, the CARCAH unit's operating hours vary and often depend on the requirements levied. Its ability to coordinate non-operational missions is extremely limited. Research missions can only be considered on a non-interference basis when flown concurrently with a tasked mission or when data collected will be directly beneficial to NHC in real time. However, CARCAH will need to have advance notification of *all* planned research missions in areas where operations are being conducted, including proposed flight tracks, aircraft altitudes, and locations where expendables may be deployed; this information can be e-mailed to ncep.nhc.carcah@noaa.gov or faxed to 305-553-1901 (please indicate "CARCAH" on faxed materials).
- IAW JO 7110.65, only 53 WRS and NOAA aircraft performing tasked

operational missions will have priority for access to the operations area.
- **Dedicated NORAD Mode 3/A Transponder Codes.** N/A.

6.1.2.2. CARCAH Pre-mission Coordination. CARCAH's pre-mission coordination procedures include:
- Publishing the TCPOD when required.
- Coordinating with the affected ARTCCs and ATCSCC as required.
- For unscheduled missions, notifying the flying units and ATCSCC.
- Notifying 53 WRS and NOAA AOC flight crews when other research missions will be airborne in the operations area at the same time.

6.1.2.3. 53 WRS and NOAA AOC Pre-mission Coordination.
- **Mission Coordination Sheet.** As soon as possible, but no later than 1-2 hours prior to departure time, fax the Mission Coordination Sheet (see Appendix L) to the ATCSCC and affected ARTCCs (see Appendix I).
- **Missions Not Listed in the TCPOD.** In the event of an unscheduled mission, the flying unit will contact the ATCSCC. The ATCSCC will initiate a conference call with the unit and all affected ARTCCs.
- **Dedicated NORAD Mode 3/A Transponder Codes.** 53 WRS and NOAA NHOP missions have dedicated NORAD mode 3/A transponder codes. These codes are only applicable in FAA controlled airspace in the Gulf of Mexico and Atlantic. They are issued by the 601st Air & Space Operations Center, Airspace Management Team (DSN 523-5837 or COM 850-283-5837) and must be renewed on an annual basis. The codes are as follows:
  - TEAL 70–79: 7552-57 & 7560-63
  - NOAA 42, 43 and 49: 5051-5054 and 5064

6.1.2.4. Mission Coordination Sheet. All missions must provide a Mission Coordination Sheet to the affected ARTCCs and the ATCSCC 1-2 hours prior to departure time (see Appendix L).

6.1.2.5. Aircraft Call Signs.
- 53 WRS: "TEAL 70 through 79" (WC-130J aircraft)
- NOAA AOC: "NOAA 42 and 43" (WP-3D aircraft); "NOAA 49" (G-IV aircraft)
- NASA: "NASA817" (DC-8 aircraft); "NASA 871 & 872" (Global Hawk UAS)
- NRL: "WARLOCK 587" (NP-3 aircraft)
- NSF/NCAR: "N677F" (G-V aircraft)

6.1.2.6. Flight Plan Filing Procedures. Flight plans must be filed with the FAA as soon as practicable before departure time. For flights into all U.S. FIRs, include delay time in the Route portion of the International Flight Plan - this will keep the IFR flight plan active throughout operations in the delay area while in FAA controlled airspace. Due to limited information that is displayed on FAA controller screens, it is recommended that only the following remarks be included in the "Other Information" block:
- "EET" to FIR boundaries,

- Navigation Performance (ex. RNP-10); and
- "RMK/MDCN" diplomatic clearance information.

6.1.2.7. Mission Cancellation. When a mission is cancelled or delayed, the unit flying the mission must notify the Primary ARTCC as soon as possible.

6.1.3. Annual Liaison Meetings.

6.1.3.1.   At a minimum, an annual liaison meeting will be conducted between the following participants: 53 WRS, NOAA AOC, the ATCSCC and affected ARTCCs. This meeting will review the previous season's operations, any proposed changes to the current NHOP, FAA liaison flights, and ICAO operations. This meeting will take place annually, normally in conjunction with the OFCM-sponsored Interdepartmental Hurricane Conference (IHC).

6.1.3.2.   Annual ARTCC and ATCSCC visits and briefings by 53 WRS and NOAA AOC aircrews and FAA Military Liaisons are encouraged. These joint visits emphasize the unique challenges and non-standard operational procedures, communication and coordination required to successfully and safely accomplish the Hurricane Hunter mission.

6.1.4. FAA Familiarization Flights. FAA Familiarization Flights on USAF (IAW AFI 11-401 and DOD 4515.13-R) and NOAA Hurricane Hunter aircraft are authorized and encouraged. These flights are important to ensure FAA controllers have a better understanding of Hurricane Hunter operations and how these missions play a vital role to inform emergency planners and coastal citizens on the storm's track and intensity as they approach the U.S. coastline.

6.2.   Mission Execution.

Note: No procedure in the NHOP precludes Aircraft Commanders from exercising their authority in the interest of safety or during an aircraft emergency.

6.2.1. NHOP Missions (At or Below FL150). NOAA and 53 WRS NHOP (and NWSOP) missions have dedicated NORAD mode 3/A transponder codes associated with call signs TEAL 70–79 (7552-57 & 7560-63) (expire 31 Dec 2012) and NOAA 42, 43, and 49 (5050-5054), respectively. Both NOAA and 53 WRS aircrews will request to be assigned their dedicated mode 3/A code on the ground or after airborne.

6.2.1.1.   Priority Handling. When requested by the aircrew, ATC will provide TEAL and NOAA aircraft priority handling. The aircraft commander will only ask for priority handling when necessary to accomplish the mission.

6.2.1.2.   International Airspace. International Airspace is defined as the Airspace beyond a Sovereign State's 12nm territorial seas limit. Beyond this limit ICAO rules apply. In International Airspace, VFR flight is not allowed at night. In Class A Controlled Airspace, aircraft must operate using IFR procedures; ATC separation is provided between IFR aircraft. In Class E Controlled Airspace, both VFR and IFR operations are allowed; separation is provided between IFR aircraft but not with VFR traffic; traffic information is provided to VFR traffic and about VFR traffic, as far as practical. In Class F and G Uncontrolled Airspace, both VFR and IFR operations are allowed. When operating in uncontrolled airspace, flight information service, which includes known traffic information, is provided and the pilot is responsible for arranging the flight to avoid other traffic (ICAO, Annex 11).

6.2.1.3. IFR Procedures and Clearance. Aircrews will conduct flight operations to the maximum extent possible utilizing IFR procedures and will not normally conduct flight operations under the provisions of "Due Regard." While entering, within, or exiting the Operational Delay Area, if the aircraft commander determines that mission, weather, and/or safety requirements dictate, then they may exercise their operational prerogative and declare "Due Regard." When conducting "Due Regard" operations, aircrews will comply with as many IFR procedures as possible. Before declaring "Due Regard," the aircrew will notify ATC of their intentions – ATC will retain flight plan information. If an aircrew is unable to notify ATC beforehand, they will inform them when able. As soon as practical, the aircrew will notify ATC that they are terminating "Due Regard" operations and request resumption of IFR services. These procedures do not preclude aircraft commanders from exercising their authority in the interest of safety or during an aircraft emergency.

6.2.1.4. Altitude Assignment and Aircraft Separation. Authorized aircraft may request to operate at a single altitude or within a block. Multiple aircraft may operate in the same vicinity but at different altitudes at the same time. In order to promote mission effectiveness, aircrews from NOAA AOC and the 53 WRS will file and request the minimum block altitudes to meet their mission requirements (i.e., do not request the block at or below FL150 if the mission can be accomplished in the block FL090-110).

- **Operations in Controlled Airspace.** While IFR, ATC will assign an altitude or a block of altitudes and provide standard vertical separation between all IFR aircraft and will provide VFR traffic advisories as far as practical. Prior to departing controlled airspace, advise ATC and state your intentions; ATC will not cancel your IFR flight plan.
- **Operations in Uncontrolled Airspace (Class F and G).** Per JO 7110.65, ATC is not authorized to assign altitudes in nor provide separation between aircraft in uncontrolled airspace. While in uncontrolled airspace, the Aircraft Commander is the IFR clearance authority. In addition, aircrews are responsible for maintaining their own separation from the surface of the sea, obstacles, and oil platforms while operating below the Minimum IFR Altitude (MIA). In Class F and G Uncontrolled Airspace, both VFR and IFR operations are allowed. When operating in uncontrolled airspace, flight information service, which includes known traffic information, is provided and the pilot is responsible for arranging the flight to avoid other traffic (ICAO, Annex 11).

[Note: When an aircraft declares "Due Regard," ATC will not be responsible for that aircraft's separation from other aircraft, but the Operational Delay Area will remain active.]

6.2.1.5. Operational Delay Area. The Operational Delay Area is ATC Assigned Airspace (ATCAA) and is a cylinder of airspace *typically* defined by a block altitude at or below FL150, with a radius of 150 nm around a set of center coordinates. The operations area may include several different classifications of airspace and environments: controlled, uncontrolled, radar contact, non-radar contact, oceanic, international airspace, domestic airspace, and/or terminal areas and may encompass several controlling agencies. This area excludes the terminal areas (Class D Airspace) depicted on the NHOP Operational Maps (see Appendix K), and any other airspace within 50 NM of the CONUS shoreline until radio contact is established with ATC. If not in radar contact within the area as shown on the NHOP Operational Maps (see Appendix K), the aircrew will make position reports in relation to designated navigational aids as requested by ATC along the coast. Any changes to the operating area will be coordinated with the primary ARTCC.

6.2.1.6. ATC Communications. The aircrew normally maintains ATC communications with only the primary ARTCC. When operating within an ATC Terminal Area depicted on the NHOP Operational Maps (see Appendix K), the aircrews will be in contact with both the primary ARTCC and the Terminal Facility if it is operating. Normally, VHF, UHF or HF radios will be used for communications with ATC, when within range. In the storm environment, HF exhibits poor propagation tendencies. When HF is unusable, satellite communications (SATCOM) may be used as a back-up (see Appendix I). IFR aircraft flying in domestic or international airspace are required to maintain continuous two-way communications with the ATC/FIR even while flying in Uncontrolled Airspace (Class F or G). Monitor the active ATC radio frequency for any traffic transiting the Area.

[Note: While in international airspace, aircrews will make periodic "Operations Normal" calls to the primary ARTCC if not in radar contact and no transmissions have been made within the previous 20–40 minutes (reference: ICAO 4444/RAC 501/12 VI, 2.1).]

6.2.1.7. Backup ARTCC Communications Procedures. CARCAH maintains contact with participating aircraft at all times and is allowed to relay ATC clearances through any means available. CARCAH is responsible for ensuring that ATC clearances, clearance requests and messages are relayed in an accurate manner. Only use this method when the aircraft or ATC is unable to contact each other.

6.2.1.8. Participating Aircraft/Aircrew Procedures. A "Participating Aircraft/Aircrew" is defined as an Aircraft, Remote Piloted Aircraft (RPA) or Unmanned Aerial System (UAS) listed in the TCPOD or conducting a tasked operational mission. CARCAH will advise aircrews when other participating aircraft, RPA or UAS will be in the operations area and brief call signs and mission information.

The following actions will be taken by the aircrews to de-conflict operations and enhance situational awareness with other participating aircraft while in the Operational Delay Area:

- Set 29.92 (inches Hg) in at least one pressure altimeter per aircraft.
- Contact (Primary: VHF 123.05 MHZ, Secondary: UHF 304.8 MHZ, Back-up: HF 4701 KHz) the other participating aircraft and confirm (as a minimum) the pressure altitude, location relative to a center point position, true heading, and operating Altitude or Block Altitude. Continue to monitor the frequency during the duration of the flight.
- Even if aircraft are cleared by ATC to operate in blocks altitudes that are 1,000 feet apart (i.e., TEAL 70 is Block 090-110 and NOAA 42 is Block 060-080), aircrews will not fly within 2,000 feet (vertical) if closer than 10NM

(using Air-to-Air TACAN and/or TCAS) of other participating aircraft operating in the same area of interest without concurrence of the other participating aircraft. **Note:** If unable to maintain assigned altitude or block, immediately notify all participating aircraft and take actions to ensure sufficient vertical and/or lateral separation is maintained or attained as soon as practical.

- While in the Operational Delay Area use: "see and avoid" operations, operating in a different operational area sector (NW, NE, SW, SE), airplane-to-airplane communication position reports, Air-to-Air TACAN, TCAS, RADAR, GPS and situational displays/maps to maintain awareness of the other aircraft's location.

6.2.1.9. Weather Dropwindsonde Instrument Release. The aircraft commander is the sole responsible party for all dropwindsonde releases or sensor activations. Aircraft commanders will ensure coordination with other participating aircraft prior to release or activation. (Examples of weather instruments are dropwindsondes and oceanographic profilers (OP)).

6.2.2. Buoy Deployment Mission. Regardless of the Designated Class of Airspace (A through G) the following rules apply:

6.2.2.1. Flight Plan. A normal IFR flight plan will be filed for this mission. The coordinates for some of the planned deployments may need to be changed while en route to adjust to the forecast track of the storm. The aircraft routing will not be altered by ATC because the buoys must exit the aircraft in a specified order and they cannot be rearranged in flight.

6.2.2.2. IFR Procedures and Clearance. It is preferred that these missions be filed and flown using IFR procedures in either controlled or uncontrolled airspace. However, with the concurrence of the aircraft commander, they may be flown VFR. If this change is made en route, ATC flight following and traffic advisories will be requested by the aircrew, and any changes to the route of flight must be relayed to ATC by the aircrew.

6.2.2.3. Altitude. Aircrews are responsible for maintaining their own clearance from the surface of the sea, obstacles, and oil platforms while operating below the Minimum IFR Altitude (MIA).

6.2.2.4. Communications. See paragraphs 6.2.1.6 – 6.2.1.7.

6.2.2.5. Participating Military Aircraft (does not apply to NOAA aircraft). If there are two or more TEAL aircraft deploying buoys in the same area at the same time, they can accept MARSA operations with each other and must relay that to ATC. This will not cancel their IFR clearance but will allow ATC to no longer be responsible for providing aircraft separation between TEAL aircraft. The TEAL aircraft must be in communication with each other and have operating TCAS on at least one of the aircraft. At least one of these aircraft will have SATCOM data relay capability on board.

6.2.2.6. Priority Handling. ATC will provide aircraft priority handling to and from the deployment area only when specifically requested by the aircrew. The aircraft commander will only ask for priority handling when necessary to accomplish the mission.

6.2.3. High Altitude Synoptic Track Missions.

6.2.3.1. Flight Plan. A normal IFR flight plan will be filed for this mission. An Altitude Reservation (ALTRV) request is not required.

6.2.3.2. NOTAM. A NOTAM will be submitted by the 53 WRS, NOAA AOC, NASA, NSF, or NRL for any High Altitude Synoptic Track mission that will release weather instruments. The NOTAM must contain individual coordinates or an area defined by coordinates for all releases. Submit NOTAM request per Appendix D procedures.

6.2.3.3. Priority Handling. ATC must provide priority handling, for TEAL and NOAA mission aircraft during Synoptic Track Missions only when specifically requested by the aircrew.

6.2.3.4. Release of Dropsondes. During NHOP missions and when operationally feasible, dropsonde instrument releases from FL 190 or higher and sensor activation must be coordinated with the appropriate ARTCC/CERAP (Combined Center/RAPCON) by advising of a pending drop or sensor activation about 10 minutes prior to the event when in direct radio contact with ATC. When ATC has radar contact with the aircraft, they will notify the aircrew of any known traffic below them that might be affected. The aircraft commander is solely responsible for release of the instrument after clearing the area by all means available.

- When contact with ATC is via ARINC, event coordination must be included with the position report prior to the point where the action will take place, unless all instrument release points have been previously relayed to the affected ATC center(s). Contact between participating aircraft must be made using the frequencies listed in paragraph 6.2.1.8., second bullet.
- During NHOP missions, approximately five (5) minutes prior to release the aircrew will broadcast in the blind on radio frequencies 121.5 MHZ and 243.0 MHZ to advise any traffic in the area of the impending drop. Pilots must not make these broadcasts if they will interfere with routine ATC communications within the vicinity of an ATC facility. The aircraft commander is responsible for determining the content and duration of a broadcast, concerning the release or sensor activation.

CHAPTER 7

SATELLITE SURVEILLANCE OF TROPICAL AND SUBTROPICAL CYCLONES

7.1. Satellites.

7.1.1. Geostationary Operational Environmental Satellite (GOES). Using modern 3-axis stabilization for orbit control, GOES-14 (GOES-East) at 75°W and GOES-15 (GOES-West) at 135°W support the operational two-GOES constellation. Independent imager and sounder instruments eliminate the need to time share, yielding an increase in spatial coverage of image and sounder data at more frequent scanning intervals. The GOES also provides higher resolution and additional spectral channels than its predecessor, affording the hydrometeorological community improvements in detection, monitoring, and analysis of developing tropical cyclones. From 135°W and 75°W, routine GOES satellite data coverage is extensive, stretching from the central Pacific through the Americas to the eastern Atlantic, including the vital breeding grounds for tropical cyclones.

Routinely, each GOES schedule provides two views of the CONUS (GOES-West view is termed PACUS) every 15 minutes. More frequent interval scans can be employed to support NOAA's warning programs, including the tracking of tropical and subtropical cyclones. Government agencies and the private sector have access to digital data transmissions directly from NOAAPORT, from NOAA's Environmental Satellite Processing Center (ESPC), or directly from GOES.

The current series of GOES satellites provide satellite data generated from full resolution imager and sounder data. Imagery at 1 and 4 km resolution is available for daytime and nighttime applications. The increased resolution of the satellite imagery is a vast improvement from previous satellites. Visible data are available at 1 km, "shortwave" infrared (channel 2 data) as well as the infrared channels 3, 4, and 5 are available at 4 km resolution. Water vapor (channel 3) is available at 4 km resolution on GOES East and West. Channel 2 (Shortwave IR) data are valuable for the detection of low clouds, fog, stratus, and surface hot spots. On GOES East, channel 6 is a 13.3 μm band at 8 km that is useful in the detection of CO_2. Channel 6 improves the measurement of the height of clouds, derived winds and volcanic ash, thus improving computer model forecasts and ash warnings to the aviation community. The digital data may be enhanced to emphasize different features as desired. A suite of digital data and environmental products is available to users in the National Weather Service (NWS); the National Environmental Satellite, Data, and Information Service (NESDIS); other Federal agencies; the academic community; and many private agencies, both national and international. These data are made available through NOAAPORT, from ESPC, the Internet, and other means such as local networks.

7.1.1.1. GOES East. GOES-East is stationed at 75°W and serves NOAA operations, to include the NHC, other Federal agencies, and the private sector. Various imager channels at higher resolutions are being utilized to monitor the intensification and movement of tropical cyclones over the Atlantic Ocean and a portion of the East Pacific. In particular, greater detail in the imagery facilitates tropical cyclone monitoring and analysis, and the use of the

GOES imager channel 2 has vastly improved the detection of low-level circulation centers at night to assist in storm positioning. Retrievals from the GOES sounder are being incorporated into NCEP's numerical models to improve model output. In addition, sounder data are being exploited to generate derived product imagery such as total precipitable water, atmospheric stability indices, surface temperatures and cloud heights.

During the 1996 hurricane season, NESDIS instituted a specialized GOES-East sounder schedule consisting of four sectors covering distinct areas of the Atlantic Ocean. Of the four sounder sectors, the CONUS sector is scanned every hour and covers the northern Gulf of Mexico and the east coast of the United States. During routine scanning operations, of the other 3 sounder sectors (the Gulf of Mexico, North Atlantic, and the East Caribbean) the Gulf of Mexico sector is designated as the "primary OCONUS" (off CONUS) sector and is scanned 4 times in a 6 hour period, while the other two sectors are only scanned once in every 6 hour period. Event driven, this "primary OCONUS" sounder sector can be changed by the NHC. The "primary" OCONUS sector provides frequent scans over the area of interest to generate vertical profiles of temperature and moisture, and additional derived environmental products such as atmospheric winds.

7.1.1.2. GOES West. GOES West is stationed at 135°W. The routine scanning mode of GOES West provides coverage of the Northern and Southern Hemisphere eastern Pacific Ocean as well as the western United States. The GOES-West satellite also supports the missions of both the NHC and the CPHC, and provides coverage of developing tropical cyclones over the East and Central Pacific. The DOD and other Federal agencies are also supported.

During the 2008 Central Pacific hurricane season, NESDIS instituted a specialized GOES-West sounder schedule consisting of additional Hawaii sectors. During routine operation, the GOES-West sounder scans two Hawaii and four North Pacific sectors. To aid in the surveillance and input of additional sounder data into hurricane models, the Central Pacific Hurricane Sector (CPHC) can request an alternate GOES-West sounder schedule that replaces two North Pacific sectors with two Hawaii sectors, allowing for four Hawaii sector scans and two North Pacific sector scans in a six-hour period.

7.1.1.3. GOES-12. GOES-12 was launched on July 23, 2001, and was operating as the GOES-East satellite until April 14, 2010. On April 26, 2010, GOES-12 began to be moved to its new station at 60° West, and is operating at that location in support of GEOSS in the Americas providing imager and sounder coverage to South America and surrounding areas. GOES-12 provides one imager scan every 15 minutes for the full South American continent, and a sounder scan every four hours. Data from GOES-12 is not processed at NESDIS.

7.1.1.4. GOES-N Series. The GOES-N Series will be used to continue and enhance the environmental monitoring and communications functions of the GOES-I thru M (GOES-8 thru 12) series of NOAA operational spacecraft. GOES-13, the first in the GOES-N series, was designed with a different spacecraft bus than the previous GOES series, and contains larger power cells. This design results in the increased accuracy in navigation and instrument radiometrics, and the operation of the imager and sounder through the satellite "eclipse" season. GOES-O and GOES-P were also procured as part of the GOES-N series contract. GOES-O was launched on June 27, 2009 and renamed GOES-14; GOES-P was launched on March 4, 2010 and was renamed GOES-15.

7.1.1.5. GOES-14. GOES-14 was launched on June 27, 2009. GOES-14 is the new GOES-East satellite as of September 12, 2012.

7.1.1.6. GOES-15. GOES-15 was launched on March 4, 2010. GOES-15 is the last of the GOES N series of satellites and is currently the operational GOES-West satellite.

7.1.2. EUMETSAT Meteosat Geostationary Satellites. Meteosat-9, launched December 21, 2005, and stationed at the Prime Meridian (0°), replaced Meteosat-8, which is stationed at 9.5° East, on April 11, 2007. It provides vital coverage of developing tropical waves off the African Coast and eastern Atlantic Ocean. Conventionally, the full disk IR, visible (VIS), and water vapor imagery have a 3 km resolution whereas a specialized VIS sector provides a maximum 1 km resolution. This visible sector has a limited scan, and will shift from the West Indian Ocean to the East Atlantic Ocean from 14:00 UTC to 01:00 UTC every day during hurricane season. This shift will ensure interests monitoring for tropical activity in the North Indian Ocean (Meteo-France) as well as the East Atlantic (NHC) will be satisfied. The digital data are transmitted to NESDIS and NCEP at the NOAA Science Center (NSC) in College Park, MD, every 15 minutes. They are also available to the NHC and the Storm Prediction Center (SPC) through an encrypted DOMestic SATellite (DOMSAT) relay and through direct transmission from ESPC. Meteosat-7, launched September 2, 1997, provides coverage for the monitoring of Indian Ocean tropical cyclone formation and development while stationed at 57° East, with Meteosat-6 at 67° East in standby status.

In December 1995, EUMETSAT, the program administrator, began encrypting digital Meteosat data 24 hours per day to regulate use within Europe. Based on international data policy agreements, U.S. non-government users are allowed access via a domestic satellite to non-encrypted Meteosat data 4 times per day at synoptic times; at other times, the data are encrypted. Hence, if quarter-hourly transmissions are required to support operational requirements, it is necessary for users to register with EUMETSAT to acquire decryption devices for installation at their local site (NOAA/DOD and other U.S. government agencies are registered).

7.1.3. MTSAT-1R. The Multifunctional Transport Satellite-1 Replacement (MTSAT-1R) was launched for the Japanese Meteorological Agency (JMA) on February 26, 2005. MTSAT-1R is located at 140° East, covering the West Pacific Ocean, East Asia, and the East Indian Ocean. MTSAT-1R is similar to GOES as it carries a 5-channel imager (one visible channel at 1 km plus four IR channels at 5 km, to include a new low-light IR channel). MTSAT-1R provides imagery for the Northern Hemisphere every 30 minutes, and JMA makes the data available to 27 countries and territories in the region. Data from MTSAT-1R is available to CONUS users via the DOMSAT or directly from ESPC and available to Pacific OCONUS users directly via downlinks in Hawaii and Guam.

7.1.4. MTSAT-2. MTSAT-2 was launched on February 18, 2006 and replaced MTSAT-1R on July 1, 2010. The transportation and communication functions of MTSAT-1R will continue to be utilized after July 1, 2010, as MTSAT-1R becomes secondary. MTSAT-2 carries a 5-channel imager with data downlink through the High Resolution Picture Transmission (HRPT) service. NOAA obtains the HRPT through the current downlink and corresponding DOMSAT uplink in Keana Point, Hawaii. MTSAT-2 is stationed at 145° East, and provides coverage for the monitoring of tropical cyclone formation and development for the West Pacific Ocean, East Asia, and the East Indian Ocean.

7.1.5. COMS. The Communication, Ocean and Meteorology Satellite (COMS) is the first operational weather and ocean satellite from The Republic of Korea. COMS was developed by the Korean Astronomical Research Institute (KARI) through contract with EADS Astrium, and carries a 5 channel imager similar to the image on board MTSAT-1R and GOES. The Korean Meteorological Administration (KMA) will operate COMS through its National Meteorological Satellite Center (NSMC) with coverage of the West Pacific and East Indian oceans. COMS's launch occurred on June 26, 2010, and operates at 128.2° East.

7.1.6. Initial Joint Polar System (IJPS). Two primary operational polar orbiting satellites, NOAA's NOAA-19 and EUMETSAT's Metop-A, provide image coverage four times a day over a respective area in 6 spectral channels (however only 5 channels can be supported at one time; channel switching is used to support the 6th channel). These satellites cross the U.S. twice per day at 12-hour intervals for each geographical area near the Equatorial crossing times listed in Table 7-2. NOAA-19 and Metop-A provide the same capabilities as previous NOAA satellites, except that the Advanced Microwave Sounding Unit–B (AMSU-B) sensor flown aboard NOAA-17 and previous polar orbiters has been replaced by the Microwave Humidity Sounder (MHS) on NOAA-19. Data are available via direct readout—high-resolution picture transmission (HRPT) or automatic picture transmission (APT)—or via central processing. Data from the Advanced Very High Resolution Radiometer (AVHRR) on NOAA-19 and the corresponding Visible Infrared Imaging Radiometer (VIIRS) on board Metop-A are available on a limited basis through the GOES distribution system (Figure 7-1). The Air Force Weather Agency (AFWA), Offutt AFB, NE, receives global data from the Advanced Scatterometer (ASCAT) on board Metop-A direct from central readout sites on a pass-by-pass basis. The Command and Data Acquisition (CDA) stations at Fairbanks, AK, and Wallops, VA, acquire recorded global area coverage data sub-sampled to a 4 km spatial resolution, and then route the data to NESDIS computer facilities in Suitland, MD, where the data are processed and distributed to the NOAA, the DOD, and private communities. Ground equipment installed at various NWS regions including Kansas City, Miami (NHC), and Monterey enable direct readout and data processing of 1.1 km resolution AVHRR and VIIRS data from NOAA-19 and Metop-A. The high resolution polar data and products generated at NHC complement other satellite data sources to support tropical mission objectives.

7.1.7. Non-NOAA Satellites. NOAA uses dedicated ground support systems to ingest and process data from select Non-NOAA satellite systems for use in operational forecasting and tropical cyclone analysis. These include data from the NASA Earth Observing System (EOS) satellites: Terra, Aqua, and Aura; CORIOLIS from the Department of Defense; Jason-2 from the joint NOAA, NASA, CNES, and EUMETSAT; and Envisat from ESA. These satellites employ multiple infrared and microwave radiometers as well as active scatterometers to assess environmental features on the ocean surface. NOAA considers these datasets non-operational, and obtains the data on a best effort basis.

7.1.8. Oceansat-2. Oceansat-2 is an Indian satellite, launched September 23, 2009, by the Indian Space Research Organisation (ISRO). Oceansat-2 is designed to study surface winds and ocean surface strata as well as other oceanic and atmospheric properties. Oceansat-2 is currently completing calibration and validation phase for certification. Oceansat-2 carries two payloads for ocean related studies, Ocean Colour Monitor (OCM) and Ku-band pencil-beam Scanning Scatterometer (SCAT). SCAT will be used to determine ocean surface level wind vectors through estimation of radar backscatter. SCAT will provide valuable ocean surface wind vector data for monitoring tropical cyclone formation and development, especially since the loss of QuikScat on November 23, 2009.

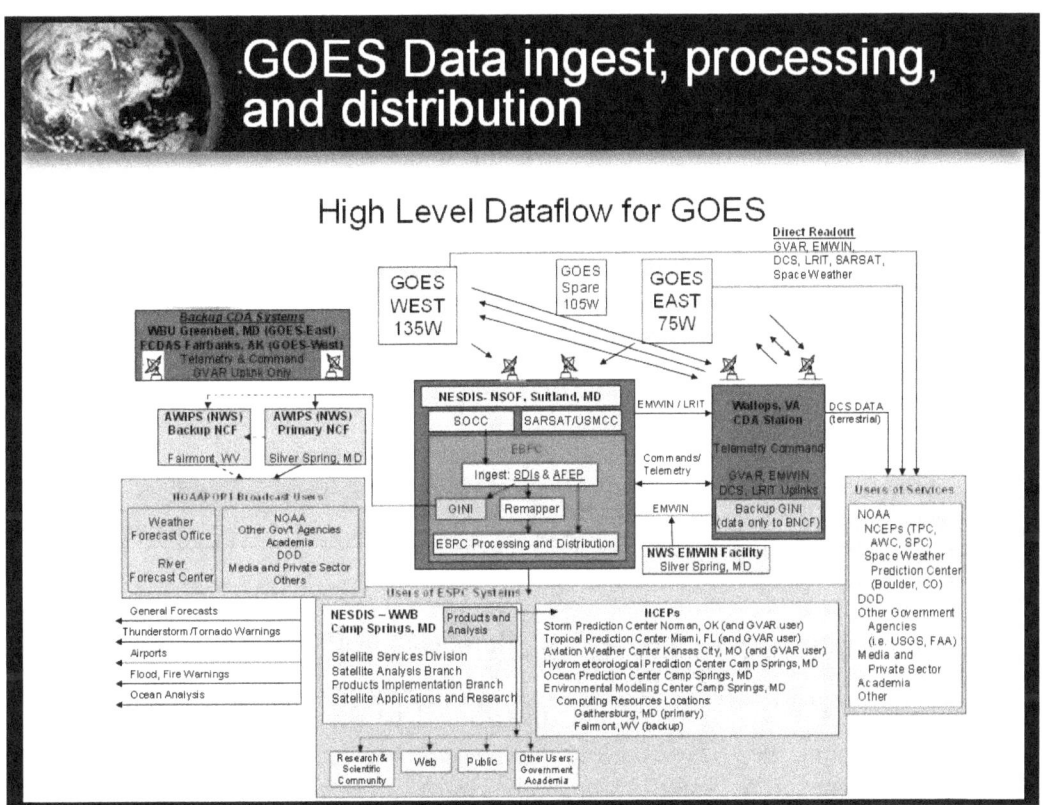

Figure 7-1. The GOES Satellite System

7.2. National Weather Service (NWS) Support.

7.2.1. Station Contacts. The GOES imagery is available in support of the surveillance of tropical and subtropical cyclones at specific NWS offices. Satellite meteorologists can be contacted at these offices; telephone numbers are in Appendix I.

7.2.2. Products. Satellite-related products are listed in Chapter 3, Table 3-5, "Summary of Products and their Associated WMO Header."

7.2.2.1. Tropical Weather Discussions. NHC issues these discussions four times a day based on satellite imagery, meteorological analysis, weather observations and radar. They describe significant features and significant weather areas for the Gulf of Mexico, the Caribbean, and between the equator and 32°N in both the Atlantic and eastern Pacific east of 140°W.

7.2.2.2. Satellite Interpretation Messages. CPHC issues these discussions four times a day to describe synoptic features and significant weather areas in the vicinity of the Hawaiian Islands. WFO Guam issues these discussions two times a day to describe synoptic features and significant weather over the Micronesian waters.

7.3   NESDIS Satellite Analysis Branch (SAB). The SAB operates 24 hours a day to provide satellite support to the WPC/OPC, NHC, CPHC, JTWC, and other worldwide users. In addition to providing high quality imagery from geostationary and polar-orbiting satellites and coordinating the execution of GOES Rapid Scan Operations (RSO) requests, SAB provides pertinent information on global tropical cyclone development, including location and intensity analysis based on the Dvorak technique (Table 7-1). For numerical model input and forecasting applications, data from high density cloud motion wind vectors, high density water vapor wind vectors, four layers of derived precipitable water from sounder moisture retrievals, and tropical rainfall estimates are provided to WPC and NHC. In addition, estimates of cumulative rainfall expected over coastal areas derived using the Ensemble Tropical Rainfall Potential (eTRaP) methodology are provided for tropical storms within 24 hours of landfall and posted to a web site in support of CPHC, WPC, NHC, forecast offices in U.S. territories, and international customers. Telephone numbers for the SAB are located in Appendix I.

Table 7-1. Communications Headings for SAB Dvorak Analysis Products

WMO HEADING	OCEANIC AREA	TYPE OF DATA
TXST20-21 KNES	South Atlantic Ocean	VIS/IR

7.4.   Air Force Support and the Defense Meteorological Satellite Program (DMSP). Data covering the National Hurricane Operations Plan areas of interest are received centrally at the Air Force Weather Agency (AFWA) and distributed to the Air Force's Operational Weather Squadrons (OWS) and the Navy's Fleet Numerical Meteorology and Oceanography Center (FNMOC) at Monterey, CA. Satellite data covering the Central Pacific area are received at or shipped to the 17th OWS Meteorological Satellite Operations (SATOPS) Flight (17 OWS/WXJ), Joint Typhoon Warning Center, Pearl Harbor, HI. The 17 OWS/WXJ uses all available meteorological satellite data when providing fix and or intensity information to Central Pacific Hurricane Center forecasters.

7.4.1.   Central Pacific Surveillance. The 17 OWS/WXJ (JTWC Satellite Operations) will provide, resources permitting, fix and intensity information to the CPHC on systems upon request.

7.5.   Satellites and Satellite Data Availability for the Current Hurricane Season. Table 7-2 lists satellite capabilities for the current hurricane season.

7.6. Current Intensity and Tropical Classification Number using the Dvorak Technique.

The current intensity (C.I.) number relates directly to the intensity of the storm. The empirical relationship between the C.I. number and a storm's wind speed is shown in Table 7-3. The C.I. number is the same as the tropical classification number (T-number) during the development stages of a tropical cyclone but is held higher than the T-number while a cyclone is weakening. This is done because a lag is often observed between the time a storm pattern indicates weakening has begun and the time when the storm's intensity decreases. An added benefit of this rule is the stability it adds to the analysis when short-period fluctuations in the cloud pattern occur. In practice, the C.I. number is not lowered until the T-number has shown weakening for 12 hours or more.

Table 7-2. Satellite and Satellite Data Availability for the Current Hurricane Season

SATELLITE	TYPE OF DATA	SCAN TIME	PRODUCTS
GOES-12 at 60°W (supporting South America) GOES-14 GOES-15	Multispectral Imager and Sounder; 5 Channels for Imager; 19 Channels for Sounder (not operational for GOES-10)	GOES-12 is providing 15 minute imager data and hourly sounder data covering South America GOES East and GOES West: Every 30 min, in Routine Scan Mode, provides 3 sectors with prescribed coverages: Northern Hemisphere (NH) or Extended NH; CONUS or PACUS; and Southern Hemisphere. Exception is transmission of full disk every 3 hours. (Available Rapid Scan Operations yield increased transmissions to 7.5 minute intervals to capture rapidly changing, dynamic weather events).	1. 1, 2, 4, and 8 km resolution visible standard sectors. 2. 4 km equivalent resolution IR sectors. 3. Equivalent and full resolution IR enhanced imagery. 4. Full disk IR every 3 hours. 5. 4 km water vapor sectors 6. Quantitative precipitation estimates; high density cloud and water vapor motion wind vectors; and experimental visible and sounder winds. 7. Operational moisture sounder data (precipitable water) in four levels for inclusion in NCEP numerical models. Other sounder products including gradient winds, vertical temperature and moisture profiles, mid-level winds, and derived product imagery (precipitable water, lifted index, and surface skin temperature). 8. Tropical storm monitoring and derivation of intensity analysis. 9. Volcanic ash monitoring and dissemination of Volcanic Ash Advisory Statements. 10. Daily northern hemisphere snow cover analysis. 11. Twice daily fire and smoke analysis over specific areas within CONUS.

Table 7-2 (continued). Satellite and Satellite Data Availability for the Current Hurricane Season

SATELLITE	TYPE OF DATA	LOCAL TIME	PRODUCTS
METEOSAT-9 at 0° (Prime Meridian) METEOSAT-8 at 9.5°E METEOSAT-7 at 57°E	Multi-spectral Spin-Scan Radiometer (SEVIRI) and High Resolution Visible (HRV)	SEVIRI: Full disk image every 15 minutes. HRV: Sector scan to move with local noon.	1. 1 km resolution digital VIS imagery (HRV); 3 km resolution digital IR imagery (SEVIRI. 2. 3 km resolution VIS and IR WEFAX imagery. 3. 3 km water vapor imagery. 4. Tropical storm monitoring and derivation of intensity analysis. 5. Volcanic ash detection and analysis.
MTSAT-1R at 140°E MTSAT-2 at 145°E	Multi-band imager (Visible plus four IR channels)	Hourly Full disk and two Northern Hemisphere scans per hour, with special "quadrant" scans four per hour.	1. 1 km resolution digital VIS imagery 2. 5 km resolution digital IR imagery and water vapor 4. Tropical storm monitoring and intensity analysis. 5. Volcanic ash detection and analysis
TRMM (NASA Tropical Rainfall Measuring Mission)	85 and 37 GHz Microwave	Fluctuates from 35°N to 35°S	1. 15 km resolution microwave coverage of the tropics from 35°S to 35°N. 2. Microwave analysis of 85 and 37 GHz radiance composited passes. 3. Brightness temperature products of the 85 and 37 GHz horizontal and vertical polarization. Derived rain-rate products.
MetOp-A NOAA-19 NOAA-18 secondary NOAA-17 backup NOAA-16 secondary NOAA-15 secondary	AVHRR; GAC and LAC (recorded); HRPT (direct); AMSU-A; AMSU-B (N-17); MHS (N-19); HIRS VIIRS 1 km global	Local Crossing Times: 0931D[1]/2131A[2] 0156D/1343A	1. 1 km resolution HRPT and Local Area Coverage (LAC) data. 2. 4 km resolution APT and Global Area Coverage (GAC) data. 3. Mapped imagery. 4. Unmapped imagery (all data types) at DMSP sites. 5. Sea-surface temperature analysis. 6. Soundings. 7. Moisture profiles. 8. Remapped GAC sectors. 9. Sounding-derived products--total precipitable water, rain rate, and surface winds under sounding 10. Daily northern hemisphere snow cover analysis. 11. Twice daily fire and smoke analysis over specific areas within CONUS. 12. AMSU based tropical cyclone intensity estimates.

[1] D - descending
[2] A - ascending

Table 7-2 (continued). Satellite and Satellite Data Availability for the Current Hurricane Season

SATELLITE	TYPE OF DATA	SCAN TIME	PRODUCTS
DMSP F-13 Tactical	OLS Imagery (recorded and direct), SSM/I, SSM/T-1	0543D[1]/1743A[2]	1. 0.3 nm (regional) and 1.5 nm (global) resolution (visual and infrared) imagery available via stored data recovery through AFWA.
DMSP F-14 Tactical	OLS Imagery (recorded and direct), SSM/I, SSM/T-1 (inop), SSM/T-2	0424D/1557A	2. Regional coverage at 0.3 nm and 1.5 nm resolution (visual and infrared) imagery available from numerous DOD tactical terminals.
DMSP F-15 Secondary	OLS Imagery (recorded and direct), SSM/I, SSM/T-1, SSM/T-2	0841D/2041A	3. SSM/T-1, SSM/T-2, SSM/I, and SSM/IS data transmitted to NESDIS and FNMOC from AFWA.
DMSP F-16 Secondary	OLS Imagery (recorded and direct), SSM/IS	0732D/1905A	
DMSP F-17 Ops	OLS Imagery (recorded and direct), SSM/IS	0528D/1728A	
DMSP F-18 Ops	OLS Imagery (recorded and direct), SSM/IS	0801D/2001A Note: Times are accurate to +/- 5 minutes	

[1] D - descending
[2] A - ascending

Table 7-3. The Dvorak Technique: The Empirical Relationship* between the C.I. Number and the Maximum Wind Speed and the Relationship between the T-Number and the Minimum Sea-Level Pressure (SLP)

C.I. NUMBER	MAXIMUM WIND SPEED	T-NUMBER	MINIMUM SLP (Atlantic)	MINIMUM SLP (NW Pacific)
1	25 kt	1		
1.5	25	1.5		
2	30	2	1009 hPa	1000 hPa
2.5	35	2.5	1005	997
3	45	3	1000	991
3.5	55	3.5	994	984
4	65	4	987	976
4.5	77	4.5	979	966
5	90	5	970	954
5.5	102	5.5	960	941
6	115	6	948	927
6.5	127	6.5	935	914
7	140	7	921	898
7.5	155	7.5	906	879
8	170	8	890	858

*Dvorak, V, 1984: Tropical Cyclone Intensity Analysis Using Satellite Data. NOAA Tech Report NESDIS 11, Wash., D.C.

CHAPTER 8

SURFACE RADAR REPORTING

8.1. **General**. Radar observations of tropical cyclones will be made at Department of Defense (DOD), National Weather Service (NWS), and Federal Aviation Administration (FAA) Weather Surveillance Radar-1988 Doppler (WSR-88D) facilities. Participating radar sites are listed in Table 8-1.

8.2. **The WSR-88D**. The WSR-88D is a computerized radar data collection and processing system. The design and implementation of the WSR-88D was a joint effort of the DOD, NWS, and FAA, and the utilization of the radar continues to be governed by tri-agency agreement. The WSR-88D is an S-band (10-cm), coherent radar, with a nominal beam width of 1 degree. The maximum data ranges are 248 nm (reflectivity) and 124 nm (velocity), although velocity data out to 162 nm can be obtained from radars using "super-resolution." Radar scanning strategies are selectable, using predetermined volume coverage patterns (VCPs). The VCP in use depends upon which weather phenomena are under surveillance. Once the radar data has been collected, it is processed automatically at the radar site by a suite of algorithms which provide graphical products for forecaster use. NHC, as an external user, obtains these products through a network connection. CPHC obtains products directly from four WSR-88Ds in Hawaii operated by the NWS Weather Forecast Office in Honolulu.

8.3. **Procedures.** As a tropical cyclone approaches, NHC uses the WSR-88D to perform radar center-fixing and to obtain other diagnostic information. Therefore, it is important to optimize WSR-88D performance for tropical cyclones and to allow other users, especially the NHC, access to radar products in the area of landfall. Most of the changes must be issued through the Master System Control Function (MSCF), Radar Product Generator (RPG) Human Computer Interface (HCI). To facilitate this process, NHC in cooperation with the Radar Operations Center (ROC) has developed an operations plan for use during tropical cyclone events. The current WSR-88D Tropical Cyclone Operations Plan is available as a sub-link to the National Hurricane Operations Plan on the OFCM web site at http://www.ofcm.gov/homepage/text/pubs.htm. It is also available via fax from the ROC Hotline (1-800-643-3363).

8.3.1. Radar Observation Requirements, WSR-88D. Chief among the requirements is the appropriate display of hurricane-force winds. Changes must be made at the radar site, guided by the WSR-88D Tropical Cyclone Operations Plan, in order to deal effectively with hurricane conditions. The physical characteristics of the tropical cyclone are best represented by use of the precipitation mode. Choice of VCP may significantly enhance (or degrade) collection of velocity data. (See WSR-88D Tropical Cyclone Operations Plan for further information.) Radar characteristics of hurricanes are given in Federal Meteorological Handbook Number 11 (FMH-11), Part B, Chapter 9. Further discussion of product usage appears in FMH-11, Part D, Unit Description and Operational Applications. A recommended product list appears in FMH-11 Part D, Application versus Product Table 4-3.

Table 8-1. Participating WSR-88D Radar Stations[1]

NWS Radars *U.S. Gulf and Atlantic Coasts*	NWS Radars *U.S. Southwest*	FAA Radars	DOD Radars
Albany, NY	Los Angeles, CA	Molokai, HI	Andersen AFB, Guam
Atlanta, GA	Phoenix, AZ	Kohala, HI	Columbus AFB, MS
Binghamton, NY	San Diego, CA	San Juan, PR	Dover AFB, DE
Birmingham, AL	Santa Ana Mtns, CA	South Hawaii, HI	Eglin AFB, FL
Boston, MA	Tucson, AZ	South Kauai, HI	Fort Hood, TX
Brandon/Jackson, MS	Yuma, AZ		Fort Polk, LA
Brownsville, TX			Fort Rucker, AL
Caribou, ME			Maxwell AFB, AL
Charleston, SC			Moody AFB, GA
Columbia, SC			Robins AFB, GA
Corpus Christi, TX			
Ft. Worth, TX			
Greer, SC			
Houston, TX			
Huntsville/Hytop, AL			
Jacksonville, FL			
Key West, FL			
Lake Charles, LA			
Melbourne, FL			
Miami, FL			
Mobile, AL			
Morehead City, NC			
New Orleans/Baton Rouge, LA			
New York City, NY			
Philadelphia, PA			
Portland, ME			
Raleigh/Durham, NC			
Roanoke, VA			
San Antonio, TX			
Shreveport, LA			
State College, PA			
Sterling, VA			
Tallahassee, FL			
Tampa, FL			
Wakefield, VA			
Wilmington, NC			

---

[1]The criterion for selection is that the radar site is located within approximately 124 nm (legacy maximum velocity range) of the coastline.

8.3.2. Central Region Report. The following fix definitions and criteria are used in reporting tropical cyclone radar observations:

- If the central region of a storm is defined by an identifiable circular, or nearly circular, wall cloud with an echo-free center, the fix (the geometric center) is reported as an "**EYE**".
- If the central region is recognizable, but not well-defined by a wall cloud (as in the case of a tropical storm), it is reported as a "**CENTER**."
- When the eye or center is only occasionally recognizable or some other central region uncertainty exists, the eye or center is reported as "**PSBL EYE**" or "**PSBL CENTER**."
- Remarks stating the degree of confidence will be included and will be classified as either "good," "fair," or "poor." If an eye is present, a "good" fix is reported when the eye is symmetrical--virtually surrounded by wall cloud; a "poor" fix is reported when the eye is asymmetrical--less than 50 percent surrounded by wall cloud; a "fair" fix is reported to express a degree of confidence between "good" and "poor." Note that a partial eyewall may be the result of excessive range from the radar, or represent the true structure of the system. Doppler velocities will, in general, increase confidence in the center position and, if available, should always be examined prior to establishing a fix.

8.3.3. Transmission of Radar Reports. When the tropical cyclone is within 200 nm of a WSR-88D, and the center fix is considered reliable, the appropriate tropical cyclone warning center (NHC or CPHC) may issue a tropical cyclone position estimate (AWIPS category TCE) between 2-hourly intermediate advisories. Note that although the issuance of this product depends upon the quality of the radar fix, other data sources such as aircraft reconnaissance may be blended with the radar estimate to obtain a position. Thus, a radar position based on particular radar may appear to disagree with the TCE position, but has in fact been taken into consideration.

- In the case of communications failure, and the event that NHC cannot obtain the necessary radar data, the local NWS Weather Forecast Office may be called upon to estimate the radar position and render qualitative assessment of the circulation.
- Other radar facilities not having weather transmission capability but wishing to provide information deemed important, should call the nearest NWS Weather Forecast Office or the NHC.

CHAPTER 9

NATIONAL DATA BUOY CAPABILITIES AND REQUIREMENTS

9.1. <u>General</u>.

9.1.1. Automated Reporting Stations. The National Data Buoy Center (NDBC) maintains automated reporting stations in the coastal and deep ocean areas of the Gulf of Mexico, the Atlantic and Pacific Oceans, and in the Great Lakes. These data acquisition systems collect real-time meteorological and oceanographic measurements for operational and research purposes. Moored buoys are deployed in the Southern Gulf of Mexico, the Caribbean and the Atlantic Ocean east of the Lesser Antilles for the primary purpose of supporting National Hurricane Center operations. NDBC also quality controls and releases meteorological data from the National Ocean Service Water Level Observing Network and from moorings and coastal stations operated by cooperating Regional Ocean Observing Systems. The NDBC website at http://www.ndbc.noaa.gov/ provides locations, latest operating status, and site-specific information for NDBC stations and provides links to details on partner organization stations. Specific questions may be addressed to NDBC Data Management and Communications Branch, Stennis Space Center, Mississippi 39529-6000, phone 228-688-2835.

9.1.2. Data Acquisition. Moored buoy and Coastal-Marine Automated Network (C-MAN) stations routinely acquire, store, and transmit data every hour; a few selected stations report more frequently. Data obtained operationally include sea level pressure, wind speed and direction, peak wind, and air temperature. Sea surface temperature and wave spectra data are measured by all moored buoys and a limited number of C-MAN stations. Relative humidity is measured at several stations. Ocean currents and salinity are measured at a few coastal stations.

NDBC acquires, encodes, and distributes data from partner organizations via NWS dissemination systems. Data from partner organizations pass through NDBC data quality control procedures prior to NWS dissemination. Frequency and timeliness of transmissions from these stations varies by organization.

9.1.3. Drifting Buoys.

9.1.3.1. NDBC. NDBC is capable of acquiring, preparing, and deploying drifting buoys; however, an operational drifting buoy requirement has not been identified or funded.

9.1.3.2. Navy. Since 1998, the Naval Oceanographic Office (NAVOCEANO) has deployed meteorological drifting buoys to report surface meteorological and oceanographic measurements, for operational purposes, as tropical systems move through data sparse regions tracking toward the U.S. East Coast. Additionally, Navy drifting buoys have been deployed in the Intertropical Convergence Zone (ITCZ). The drifting buoy measurements, which are available to tropical forecasters, provide invaluable input for defining tropical storm movement and intensity, improve forecast model initialization, and give tropical forecasters a much better sense of storm characteristics and track as they approach the fleet concentration areas of

Jacksonville, FL, and Norfolk, VA. Drifting buoys typically have a life span of 1 to 2 years, and the data are available through the NAVOCEANO homepage and through standard World Meteorological Organization (WMO) data sources.

NAVOCEANO acquires, prepares, and deploys drifting meteorological buoys based on operational requirements identified by the Commander, U.S. Atlantic Fleet (COMLANTFLT). Currently, COMLANTFLT has identified the Navy's drifting buoy support as a standing requirement to support fleet safety, assist in fleet sortie decisions, and enhance tropical weather preparedness.

9.2. **Requests for Drifting Buoy Deployment.** Drifting buoy deployments should be coordinated through the Department of Commerce (DOC), National Oceanic and Atmospheric Administration (NOAA). Deployments will be requested through the Office of the Federal Coordinator for Meteorology (OFCM) to HQ Air Force Reserve Command (AFRC). Deployments in advance of a U.S. land-threatening hurricane require a 36- to 48-hour notification.

9.2.1. CARCAH. CARCAH will issue, through the Tropical Cyclone Plan of the Day (TCPOD), an alert or outlook for drifting buoy deployment 48 hours before the planned deployment. Hard tasking for the deployment will be issued via the TCPOD at least 16 hours, plus flying time to the deployment location, before the event.

9.2.2. Deployment of Buoys. DOC may request the deployment of a drifting buoy and subsurface float array with up to 40 elements at a distance of 200 to 400 nm from the storm center, depending on the dynamics of the storm system. DOC will ensure the buoys and mission-related DOC personnel are delivered to AFRC. The specific DOC request for placement of the buoys will depend on several factors, including:

- Characteristics of the storm, including size, intensity, and velocity.
- Storm position relative to the coast and population centers.
- Availability of aircraft and *Loadmasters (LM)* certified for buoy deployment.

9.2.3. Deployment Position. The final deployment position will be provided before the flight crew briefing. An example of a possible buoy and float deployment pattern from the recent CLBAST Experiment is shown in Figure 9-1.

9.3. **Communications.** Moored buoy and C-MAN data are transmitted via NOAA Geostationary Operational Environmental Satellite (GOES) to the National Environmental Satellite, Data, and Information Service (NESDIS) or via the Iridium satellite communication system and then are relayed to the NWS Telecommunications Gateway (NWSTG) for processing and dissemination. Data from partner organizations acquired by NDBC are relayed to the NWSTG for processing and dissemination. Moored buoy observations are formatted into the World Meteorological Organization (WMO) FM13 SHIP code. C-MAN and other partner organization coastal station data are formatted into C-MAN code, which is very similar to the WMO FM12 SYNOP code. Drifting buoys transmit data via NOAA's Polar Orbiting Environmental Satellites (POES) to the U.S. Argos Global Processing Center, Largo, Maryland.

Service Argos processes and formats the data into WMO FM18 BUOY code. The messages are then routed to the NWSTG for distribution. The formats for WMO encoded messages may be found in the WMO Manual on Codes Volume One, WMO-No. 306.

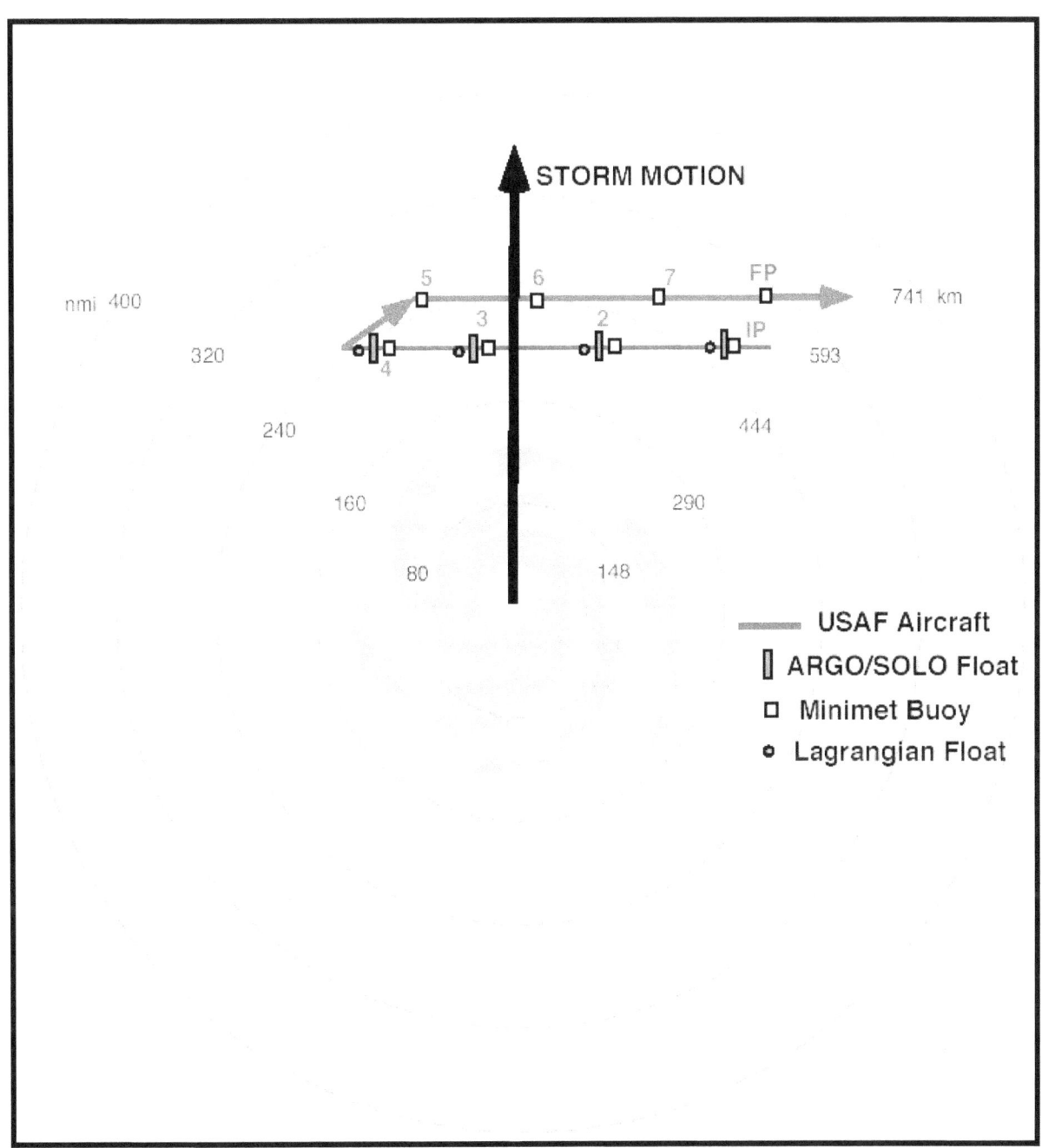

Figure 9-1. Example Buoy and Float Deployment Pattern

CHAPTER 10

MARINE WEATHER BROADCASTS

10.1. <u>General</u>. The National Weather Service and the Department of Homeland Security's United States Coast Guard (USCG) broadcast forecast products that include information on tropical cyclones issued by the National Hurricane Center and the Central Pacific Hurricane Center. The broadcast of these products supports the U.S. participation in the Global Maritime Distress and Safety System, which provides the communications support to the International Maritime Organization's (IMO) global search and rescue plan.

10.2. <u>Global Maritime Distress and Safety System (GMDSS)</u>. The goals of GMDSS are to provide more effective and efficient emergency and safety communications, and to disseminate maritime safety information to all ships on the world's oceans regardless of location or atmospheric conditions. These goals are defined in the International Convention for the Safety of Life at Sea (SOLAS) 1974, as amended. GMDSS is based upon a combination of satellite and terrestrial radio services and has changed international distress communications from being primarily ship-to-ship based to ship-to-shore (rescue coordination center) based. GMDSS provides for automatic distress alerting and locating, and requires ships to receive broadcasts of maritime safety information which could prevent a distress from happening in the first place. The NWS participates directly in the GMDSS by preparing weather forecasts and warnings for broadcast via two primary GMDSS systems--NAVTEX and Inmarsat-C SafetyNET.

10.2.1. NAVTEX. NAVTEX is an international, automated system for instantly distributing maritime navigational warnings, weather forecasts and warnings, search and rescue notices, and similar information to ships. It has been designated by the IMO as the primary means for transmitting coastal urgent marine safety information to ships worldwide. NAVTEX is broadcast from the 12 USCG stations. Coverage is reasonably continuous along the east, west, and Gulf coasts of the United States, as well as the area around Kodiak, Alaska, Guam, and Puerto Rico. Typical NAVTEX transmissions range from 200-400 nm.

10.2.2. SafetyNET. Satellite systems operated by Inmarsat Ltd. are an important element of the GMDSS. Inmarsat-C provides ship/shore, shore/ship, and ship/ship store-and-forward data and telex messaging; the capability for sending preformatted messages to a rescue coordination center; and the SafetyNET service. The Inmarsat-C SafetyNET service is a satellite-based worldwide maritime safety information broadcast service of high seas weather warnings, navigational warnings, radionavigation warnings, ice reports and warnings generated by USCG-conducted International Ice Patrol, and other information not provided by NAVTEX.

10.3. <u>Coastal Maritime Safety Broadcasts</u>. In addition to NAVTEX, the USCG and other government agencies broadcast maritime safety information, using a variety of different radio systems to ensure coverage of different ocean areas for which the United States has responsibility and to ensure all ships of every size and nationality can receive this vital safety information.

10.3.1. VHF Marine Radio. The USCG broadcasts nearshore and storm warnings of interest to the mariner on VHF channel 22A (157.1 MHZ) following an initial call on the distress, safety, and calling channel 16 (156.8 MHZ). Broadcasts are made from over 200 sites, covering the coastal areas of the U.S., including the Great Lakes, major inland waterways, Puerto Rico, Alaska, Hawaii, and Guam. All ships in U.S. waters over 20 meters in length are required to monitor VHF channel 16 and must have radios capable of tuning to the VHF simplex channel 22A. Typical coverage is 25 nm offshore.

10.3.2. Medium Frequency Radiotelephone (Voice). The USCG broadcasts offshore forecasts and storm warnings of interest to mariners on 2670 kHz, after first being announced on the distress, safety, and calling frequency 2182 kHz.

10.3.3. NOAA Weather Radio. The NOAA Weather Radio network continually broadcasts coastal and marine forecasts on frequencies near 162 MHZ. Recorded voice broadcasts have largely been supplanted by a synthesized voice. The network provides near-continuous coverage of the coastal U.S., Great Lakes, Hawaii, Guam, Commonwealth of the Northern Mariana Islands, and the populated Alaska coastline. Typical coverage is 25 nm offshore.

10.4.   High Seas Broadcasts. NWS high seas weather forecasts and warnings are also available on the following high frequency (HF) broadcasts.

10.4.1. HF Radiotelephone (Voice). Weather forecasts and warnings for high seas and offshore areas are broadcast over scheduled HF single sideband (SSB) radiotelephone channels from USCG communications stations using a very distinctive and recognizable computer-synthesized voice.

10.4.2. HF Radiofacsimile. The USCG broadcasts NWS high seas weather maps from five communications stations--Boston, MA (NMF); Point Reyes, CA (NMC); New Orleans, LA (NMG), Honolulu, HI (KVM-70) (a DOD station); and Kodiak, AK (NOJ). Limited satellite imagery, sea surface temperature maps, and text forecasts are also available.

10.4.3. HF Radiotelex (HF SITOR). High seas forecasts in text format, recognized by the GMDSS, are broadcast over scheduled GMDSS HF narrow-band direct printing channels from USCG communications stations. Limited offshore forecasts are also available.

10.4.4. WWV, WWVH HF Voice (Time Tick). Atlantic high seas warnings are broadcast at 7 and 8 minutes past the hour over WWV (Boulder, CO) on the following HF frequencies: 2.5, 5, 10, 15, and 20 MHZ; Pacific high seas warnings are broadcast at 9 minutes past the hour. Pacific high seas warnings are broadcast from 48-51 minutes past the hour over WWVH (Honolulu, HI) at 2.5, 5, 10, and 15 MHZ. These are the National Institute of Standards and Technology (NIST) standard time/frequency broadcasts.

10.5. **Additional Information**.   Further information concerning these and other marine broadcasts, including schedules, frequencies, and links to products can be found at:

- www.nws.noaa.gov/om/marine/home.htm
- http://www.navcen.uscg.gov/?pageName=maritimeTelecomms

In addition, the National Geospatial-Intelligence Agency (NGA), Publication 117, Radio Navigational Aids (http://msi.nga.mil/NGAPortal/MSI.portal; click on "Publications;" from Menu Options, select "Radio Navigational Aids"), contains detailed information on maritime safety information broadcasts within the U.S. and worldwide.

CHAPTER 11

PUBLICITY

11.1. **News Media Releases.** News media releases, other than warnings and advisories, for the purpose of informing the public of the operational and research activities of the Departments of Commerce, Defense, and Transportation should reflect the joint effort of these agencies by giving due credit to the participation of other agencies.

11.2. **Distribution.** Copies of these releases should be forwarded to the following agencies:

- NOAA Office of Public Affairs
  Herbert C. Hoover Building
  14th and Constitution Avenue, N.W.
  Washington, DC 20230

- Commander, Naval Meteorology and Oceanography Command
  1100 Balch Boulevard
  Stennis Space Center, MS 39522-3001

- HQ Air Force Reserve Command (AFRC/PA)
  Robins AFB, GA 31093

- Joint Staff Weather Officer
  The Joint Chiefs of Staff (J3/DDGO-ROD)
  Pentagon Room 2D-921G
  Washington, DC 20318-3000

- Federal Aviation Administration (APA-310)
  800 Independence Avenue, S.W.
  Washington, DC 20591

- Director, NOAA Aircraft Operations Center
  P.O. Box 6829
  MacDill AFB, FL 33608-0829

- Federal Coordinator for Meteorology
  Suite 1500, 8455 Colesville Road
  Silver Spring, MD 20910

APPENDIX A

LOCAL NATIONAL WEATHER SERVICE (NWS) OFFICE PRODUCTS

A.1. **General**. This appendix briefly describes some of the products issued by local National Weather Service (NWS) offices which support the tropical cyclone forecasting and warning program. Additional details of all the products can be found in National Weather Service Instruction 10-601, located at http://www.weather.gov/directives.

A.2. **Products.**

A.2.1. Hurricane/Typhoon Local Statements (HLS). WFOs with coastal county responsibilities and selected inland WFOs will issue these products which are very specific and designed to inform media, local decision makers, and the public on present and anticipated storm effects in their county warning area (CWA) and adjacent coastal waters. HLSs will add localized details to tropical cyclone center's advisory releases and should not conflict with or repeat advisory information not directly applicable to the local office's CWA.

Coastal WFOs are defined as those having at least one county with significant tidal influences. Those are:

EASTERN REGION	SOUTHERN REGION	WESTERN REGION	PACIFIC REGION

Caribou, ME
Portland, ME
Boston, MA
New York City, NY
Philadelphia, PA
Baltimore, MD/
    Washington, DC
Wakefield, VA
Newport/
    Morehead City,
NC
Wilmington, NC
Charleston, SC
	Brownsville, TX
	Corpus Christi, TX
	Houston/Galveston,
	TX
	Lake Charles, LA
	New Orleans, LA
	Mobile, AL
	Tallahassee, FL
	Tampa Bay, FL
	Miami, FL
	Key West, FL
	Melbourne, FL
	Jacksonville, FL
	San Juan, PR
		San Diego, CA
		Los Angeles/
		    Oxnard, CA
			Honolulu, HI
			Guam
			WSO Pago Pago,
			    American Samoa

A.2.2. Extreme Wind Warning (EWW). Short duration warnings are issued by WFOs to protect lives and property. WFO forecasters issue short duration EWW products to provide the public with advance notice of the onset of extreme tropical cyclone winds, usually associated with the eyewall of a major (category 3 or higher) tropical cyclone. Extreme Wind Warnings inform the public of the need to take immediate shelter in an interior portion of a well-built structure due to the onset of extreme tropical cyclone winds.

A.2.3. Post-Tropical Cyclone Reports (PSH). The PSH is the primary WFO post tropical cyclone product issued to the public to report and document local tropical cyclone impacts. The PSH product is intended to provide the NHC, NWS Headquarters, the media, the public, and emergency management officials with a record of peak tropical cyclone conditions. This data is then used to formulate other post-event reports, news articles and historical records.

APPENDIX B

DEFINING POINTS FOR TROPICAL CYCLONE WATCHES/WARNINGS

The coastal areas placed under tropical storm and hurricane/typhoon watches and warnings are described through the use of "breakpoints" or geographical positions. The National Weather Service (NWS) designates the locations along the U.S. East, Gulf, and California coasts, Puerto Rico, and Hawaii. Individual countries across the Caribbean, Central America, and South America provide coastal locations for their areas of responsibility to the NWS for the National Hurricane Center's use in tropical cyclone advisories when watches/warnings are issued by international partners. For graphical representations of the breakpoints, see http://www.nhc.noaa.gov/breakpoints_graphics.shtml. An additional source for breakpoint information is NWS Instruction 10-605, located at http://www.weather.gov/directives.

APPENDIX C

JOINT TYPHOON WARNING CENTER (JTWC) BULLETINS

Below are the abbreviated communications headers and titles for the products for which JTWC is responsible. A brief description of each product, to include scheduled transmission times, is available http://www.usno.navy.mil/JTWC/products-and-services-notice.

ABIO10 PGTW	Significant Weather Advisory, Indian Ocean
ABPW10 PGTW	Significant Weather Advisory, Western Pacific Ocean
WTPN21-26 PGTW	Tropical Cyclone Formation Alert, Northwest Pacific Ocean
WTPN31-36 PGTW	Tropical Cyclone Warning, Northwest Pacific Ocean
WDPN31-36 PGTW	Prognostic Reasoning Bulletin, Northwest Pacific Ocean
WTIO21-25 PGTW	Tropical Cyclone Formation Alert, North Indian Ocean
WTIO31-35 PGTW	Tropical Cyclone Warning, North Indian Ocean
WTPS21-25 PGTW	Tropical Cyclone Formation Alert, Southwest Pacific Ocean
WTPS31-35 PGTW	Tropical Cyclone Warning, Southwest Pacific Ocean
WTXS21-26 PGTW	Tropical Cyclone Formation Alert, South Indian Ocean
WTXS31-36 PGTW	Tropical Cyclone Warning, South Indian Ocean
WTPN21-25 PHNC	Tropical Cyclone Formation Alert, Northeast Pacific Ocean
WTPN31-35 PHNC	Tropical Cyclone Warning, Northeast Pacific Ocean
FKPN31-35 PHNC	Prognostic Reasoning Bulletin, Northeast Pacific Ocean
WTPS21-25 PHNC	Tropical Cyclone Formation Alert, Southeast Pacific Ocean
WTPS31-35 PHNC	Tropical Cyclone Warning, Southeast Pacific Ocean
TPPN10-19 PGTW	Tropical Cyclone Position and Intensity, Northwest Pacific Ocean
TPIO10-19 PGTW	Tropical Cyclone Position and Intensity, North Indian Ocean
TPPS10-19 PGTW	Tropical Cyclone Position and Intensity, Southwest Pacific Ocean
TPXS10-19 PGTW	Tropical Cyclone Position and Intensity, Southern Indian Ocean
TPPZ01-05 PGTW	Tropical Cyclone Position and Intensity, Central North Pacific Ocean

APPENDIX D

FORMAT FOR NHOP/NWSOP FLIGHT INFORMATION FOR INTERNATIONAL AND DOMESTIC NOTAM ISSUANCE

Flight information shall be sent to the NOTAM office via facsimile for dissemination as an International and Domestic NOTAM in the following format (Note: The request is made for a domestic NOTAM which will then automatically makes its way into the international NOTAM system):

HEADER
Request a Domestic NOTAM be Issued

A.   Affected Center(s). This field will include all affected ARTCCs in 3-letter identifier format; e.g., ZNY, ZOA, ZAN. Synoptic track flights will probably utilize more than one ARTCC, and any adjacent ARTCC should be included when the flight track is within 100 miles of the adjacent center's airspace. Flights that are flying in the storm environment will utilize the ARTCC whose airspace is mostly affected.

B.   Start Time (YYMMDDZZZZ). For example, 0006011600. This time would correspond to the entry time on a reconnaissance track or time at the storm fix latitude/longitude.

C.   Ending Time (YYMMDDZZZZ). This would be the completion time of reconnaissance track or the time exiting the storm environment.

E.*   Text. This field is free form and should include the following information: route of flight for the <u>mission portion</u> (latitude/longitude, fixes, airways), type of activity (laser, dropsonde, etc.), frequency/location of deployment, broadcast frequencies, any other pertinent information that may concern other flights. Include a unit/agency phone number and point of contact for possible questions.

F.   Lower Altitude (during mission). Use "Surface" since the dropsonde is the "reason" for the NOTAM as much or more so than the aircraft altitude.

G.   Upper Altitude (during mission). For example, FL450.

      If only one altitude is to be used, then F and G may be combined. If altitude is going to vary throughout the mission, utilize "see text" and the information can be inserted there and the altitudes may be explained in field E.

      * Note that there is no paragraph "D". It is reserved for FAA use.

      NOTES:
      1. Only ICAO approved contractions may be used.
      2. Using this format will help ensure timely and accurate information dissemination.

APPENDIX E

SAFFIR-SIMPSON HURRICANE WIND SCALE

<u>Saffir-Simpson Hurricane Wind Scale:</u> The Saffir-Simpson Hurricane Wind Scale (SSHWS) is a scale on a 1 to 5 categorization based on the hurricane's intensity at the indicated time. The scale provides examples of the type of damages and impacts associated with winds of the indicated intensity. In general, damage rises by a factor of four for every category increase. The maximum sustained surface wind peak (peak 1-minute wind at the standard meteorological observation height of 10 m [33 ft] over unobstructed exposure) associated with the cyclone is the determining factor in the scale. (Note that sustained winds can be stronger in hilly or mountain terrain compared with that experienced over flat terrain). Details for the Atlantic and Eastern Pacific Hurricane Basins and Central Pacific Hurricane Basin regarding the SSHWS can be found at the web sites indicated below.

Atlantic and Eastern Pacific Hurricane Basins: http://www.nhc.noaa.gov/aboutsshs.shtml.

Central Pacific Hurricane Basin: http://www.prh.noaa.gov/cphc/pages/aboutsshs.php.

APPENDIX F

OFFICIAL INTERAGENCY AGREEMENTS

The following enclosure is the Memorandum of Agreement (MOA) between the Air Force Reserve Command (AFRC) and the National Oceanic and Atmospheric Administration (NOAA), October 12, 2000. The purpose of this agreement is to establish policies, principles, and procedures under which the AFRC and NOAA provide aircraft weather reconnaissance and surveillance in support of NOAA's tropical cyclone forecast, warning, and research missions.

MEMORANDUM OF AGREEMENT

BETWEEN

THE UNITED STATES AIR FORCE RESERVE COMMAND

AND

THE NATIONAL OCEANIC AND ATMOSPHERIC ADMINISTRATION

PURPOSE: The National Oceanic and Atmospheric Administration (NOAA), an agency of the Department of Commerce, does not have the capability to fully support all operational requirements in support of tropical cyclone and winter storm aerial reconnaissance. This memorandum of agreement establishes policies, principles, and procedures under which the Air Force Reserve Command (AFRC) will provide aircraft weather reconnaissance support to NOAA. NOAA and AFRC enters into this agreement pursuant to its authority under 15 U.S.C. 313.

1. REFERENCES:

   a. *National Hurricane Operations Plan* (NHOP)

   b. *National Winter Storms Operations Plan* (NWSOP)

   c. Department of Defense Appropriations Act, 2000

2. BACKGROUND: The Air Force Reserve Command (AFRC) maintains 10 WC-130s to meet the Department of Commerce (DOC) aircraft reconnaissance requirements. AFRC will conduct up to five (5) sorties per day in support of NHOP requirements and up to two (2) sorties per day in support of NWSOP requirements. The Department of Defense (DOD), through AFRC, will bear all costs directly attributed to providing aircraft weather reconnaissance support. Support will be limited to the number of AFRC congressionally funded aircraft flying hours per year.

   a. Total flying hours used to support the weather reconnaissance mission are set annually in the DOD Appropriations Act. The 53rd Weather Reconnaissance Squadron (53 WRS) manages the flying hour program.

   b. The operational area for AFRC weather reconnaissance includes the Atlantic Ocean, Gulf of Mexico, the Caribbean Sea, and the North Pacific Ocean east of the international date line, as outlined in the NHOP and the NWSOP.

   c. The 53 WRS will be capable of operating from two (2) deployed locations, as well as from home station, simultaneously, supporting a maximum of five tropical cyclone sorties per day or two winter storm sorties per day.

3. <u>IMPLEMENTATION</u>: Implementation details are contained in "GENERAL PROVISIONS."

4. <u>GENERAL PROVISIONS</u>:

   a. AFRC agrees:

      1) Within the limits of military capability, to meet NOAA's requirements for aerial weather reconnaissance in accordance with the NHOP and NWSOP.

      2) To provide at the Tropical Prediction Center/National Hurricane Center (TPC/NHC) the staff and equipment required to support the mission of the Chief, Aerial Reconnaissance Coordination, All Hurricanes (CARCAH). CARCAH provides 24-hour telecon/aircraft SATCOM operational interface between NOAA/TPC/NHC and AFRC/53WRS for NHOP and NWSOP taskings. CARCAH is a subunit of and reports directly to the 53WRS.

   b. NOAA agrees to promptly notify AFRC/53WRS of the requirements for tropical cyclone or winter storm mission taskings in accordance with the NHOP and the NWSOP. Tropical cyclone missions will be tasked by the Director, TPC/NHC. Winter storm missions will be tasked by the Director, National Centers for Environmental Prediction.

   c. AFRC recognizes the obligation to support winter storm operations and associated research projects as delineated by the DOD Appropriations Act and the NWSOP. Support to research projects will be contingent upon aircraft availability.

5. <u>MOBILIZATION</u>: In times of national emergency or war, some or all AFRC/53WRS reconnaissance resources may not be available to fulfill DOC/NOAA needs.

6. <u>EFFECTIVE AND TERMINATION DATES</u>: This memorandum will become effective on the date signed by the last approving official. The parties will review this memorandum of agreement at least once every three years to determine whether it should be revised, amended, or cancelled. Amendments or revisions to this agreement require the mutual consents of the parties.

7. <u>COORDINATION</u>:

The agency contacts for coordination of the activities under this MOU are:

AOC: CAPT Robert W. Maxson, NOAA, Aircraft Operations Center, DOC, MacDill AFB, Florida; phone: (813) 828-3310 ext. 3001; fax: (813) 828-3266 E-mail Bob.W.Maxson@NOAA.gov

Ms. Julie Robertson, (813) 828-3310 ext. 3010; fax: (813) 828-8923 E-mail
Julie.A.Robertson@NOAA.gov

AFRC:

HQ AFRC/DOOX
DSN 497-1161; Commercial (228)327-1161

403 WG/XPL
SSgt Clarence Hester Jr., Logistics Plans Manager
Keesler AFB, MS
DSN 597-3521; Commercial (228) 377-3521
Fax DSN 597-4624; Commercial (228) 377-3521
Email: Clarence.Hester@keesler.af.mil

53 WRS
Lt Col Dennis L. Price, Director of Operation
817 H Street, Keesler AFB, MS 39534
DSN 597-8510; Commercial (228) 377-8510
Fax DSN 597-1923; Commercial (228) 337-1923
Email: Dennis.Price@keesler.af.mil

8. RESOLUTION OF DISAGREEMENTS

Nothing herein is intended to conflict with current DOC or the NOAA Aircraft Operations
Center directives. If the terms of this agreement are inconsistent with existing directives of
either of the agencies entering into this agreement, then those portions of this agreement
which are determined to be inconsistent shall be invalid, but the remaining terms and
conditions not affected by the inconsistency shall remain in full force and effect. At the first
opportunity for review of the agreement, all necessary changes will be accomplished either by
an amendment to this agreement or by entering into a new agreement, whichever is deemed
expedient to the interest of both parties.

Should disagreement arise on the interpretation of the provisions of this agreement, or
amendments and/or revisions thereto, that cannot be resolved at the operating level, the
area(s) of disagreement shall be stated in writing by each party and presented to the other
party for consideration. If agreement on interpretation is not reached within thirty (30) days,
the parties shall forward the written presentation of the disagreement to respective higher
officials for appropriate resolution.

FOR THE UNITED STATES
AIR FORCE RESERVE COMMAND

FOR THE NATIONAL OCEANIC AND
ATMOSPHERIC ADMINISTRATION

RWMaxson Capt NOAA

Date: _2 Oct 2000_

Date: _10/12/2000_

APPENDIX G

RECCO, HDOB, AND TEMP DROP

CODES, TABLES, AND REGULATIONS

Figure G-1. Reconnaissance Code Recording Form

DATE | ORGANIZATION | MISSION IDENTIFIER

	1	2	3	4	5	6	7	8
NUMBER	9	g	Y	L_o	h_a	d	T	I
	X — RECCO INDICATOR SPECIFYING TYPE OF OBSERVATION (Table 1)	g — TIME OF OBSERVATION (Hours and Minutes) (GMT)	Q — OCTANT (Table 3)	L_o — LONGITUDE DEGREES AND TENTHS (Note 4)	h_a — PRESSURE ALTITUDE OF AIRCRAFT REPORTED TO THE NEAREST DECAMETER	d — WIND DIRECTION AT FLIGHT LEVEL (Tens of deg. true)	T — TEMPERATURE WHOLE °C (Note 6)	I_i — INDEX TO HHH (Table 9)
	X	g	L_a	L_o	h_a	f	T_d	H
	X (Table 1)	g	L_a — LATITUDE DEGREES AND TENTHS	B — TURBULENCE (Table 4)	d_t — TYPE OF WIND (Table 6)	f — WIND SPEED AT FLIGHT LEVEL (Knots)	T_d — DEW POINT WHOLE °C (Note 8)	H — GEOPOTENTIAL HEIGHT/ D-VALUE OR SLP PER INDEX i
OBSERVATION	9	I_d — DEW POINT INDICATOR (Table 2)	L_a	f_c — FLIGHT COND (Table 5) (Note 5)	d_a — METHOD OF OBTAINING WIND (Table 7)	f	w — PRESENT WEATHER (Note 7 Table 8)	H (Note 8)

REMARKS

TYPE AIRCRAFT | CALL SIGN | METEOROLOGIST

	9	10	11	12	13	14	15	16
	1 — INDICATOR	c — CLOUD TYPE (Table 11)	c — CLOUD TYPE (Table 11)	c — CLOUD TYPE (Table 11)	1 — INDICATOR	c — CLOUD TYPE (Table 11)	c — CLOUD TYPE (Table 11)	c — CLOUD TYPE (Table 11)
	k_n — NR OF CLOUD LAYERS (Note 9)	h_s — ALTITUDE OF BASE	h_s — ALTITUDE OF BASE	h_s — ALTITUDE OF BASE	K_n — NR OF CLOUD LAYERS (Note 9)	h_s — ALTITUDE OF BASE	h_s — ALTITUDE OF BASE	h_s — ALTITUDE OF BASE
	N_s — AMOUNT OF CLOUDS (Note 9) Table 10	h_s (Table 12)	h_s (Table 12)	h_s (Table 12)	N_s — AMOUNT OF CLOUDS (Note 9) Table 10	h_s (Table 12)	h_s (Table 12)	h_s (Table 12)
	N_s	H_t — ALTITUDE OF TOP (Table 12)	H_t — ALTITUDE OF TOP (Table 12)	H_t — ALTITUDE OF TOP (Table 12)	N_s	H_t — ALTITUDE OF TOP (Table 12)	H_t — ALTITUDE OF TOP (Table 12)	H_t — ALTITUDE OF TOP (Table 12)
	N_s	H_t	H_t	H_t	N_s	H_t	H_t	H_t

REMARKS

RECCO RECORDING WORKSHEET

	17	18	19	20	21	22	23	24	
	4 — INDICATOR	6 — INDICATOR (Note 11)	6 — INDICATOR (Note 11)	7 — INDICATOR	7 — INDICATOR	8 — INDICATOR	8 — INDICATOR	9 — INDICATOR	
	d — DIRECTION OF SFC WIND (Tens of deg. true)	W_s — SIGNIFICANT WEATHER CHANGES (Table 14)	W_s — SIGNIFICANT WEATHER CHANGES (Table 14)	I_r — RATE OF ICING (Table 17)	h_i — ALT OF BASE OF ICING STRATUM (Note 12)	d_r — BEARING OF ECHO CENTER	E_w — ECHO WIDTH OR DIAMETER (Table 19)	V_i — INFLIGHT VISIBILITY (Table 23)	
	d	S_s — DISTANCE OF OCCURENCE OF Ws (Table 15)	S_s — DISTANCE OF OCCURENCE OF Ws (Table 15)	I_t — TYPE OF ICING (Table 18)	h_i — ALTITUDE OF TOP OF ICING STRATUM (Table 19)	d_r — (Tens of Deg. True)	E_l — LENGTH OF MAJ AXIS (Table 19)	T_w — SEA SURFACE TEMPERATURE DEGREES AND TENTHS	REMARKS
	f — SURFACE WIND SPEED (knots) (Note 10)	w_d — DISTANT WEATHER (Table 16)	w_d — DISTANT WEATHER (Table 16)	S_b — DISTANCE TO BEGINNING OF ICING (Table 15)	H_i — DISTANCE TO TOP OF ICING STRATUM	S_r — DISTANCE TO ECHO CENTER (Table 19)	c_e — CHARACTER OF ECHO (Table 21)	T_w	
	f	d_w — BEARING OF W_d (Table 13)	d_w — BEARING OF W_d (Table 13)	S_e — DISTANCE TO ENDING OF ICING (Table 15)	H_i — (Note 12) (Table 12)	O_e — ORIENTATION OF ELLIPSE (Table 20)	i_e — INTENSITY OF ECHO (Table 22)	T_w	

REMARKS

Table G-1. Reconnaissance Code Tables

TABLE 1 XXX
222	Sec One Observation without radar capability
555	Sec Three (intermediate) observation with or without radar capability
777	Sec One Observation with radar capability

TABLE 2 i_d
0	No dew point capability/acft below 10,000 meters
1	No dew point capability/acft at or above 10,000 meters
2	No dew point capability/acft below 10,000 meters and flight lvl temp -50 C or colder
3	No dew point capability/acft at or above 10,000 meters and flight lvl temp -50 C or colder
4	Dew point capability/acft below 10,000 meters
5	Dew point capability/acft at or above 10,000 meters
6	Dew point capability/acft below 10,000 meters and flight lvl temp -50 C or colder
7	Dew point capability/acft at or above 10,000 meters and flight lvl temp -50 C or colder

TABLE 3 Q
0	0 -90 W	Northern
1	90 W - 180	Northern
2	180 - 90 E	Northern
3	90 - 0 E	Northern
4	Not Used	
5	0 - 90 W	Southern
6	90 W - 180	Southern
7	180 - 90 E	Southern
8	90 - 0 E	Southern

TABLE 4 B
0	None
1	Light turbulence
2	Moderate turbulence in clear air, infrequent
3	Moderate turbulence in clear air, frequent
4	Moderate turbulence in cloud, infrequent
5	Moderate turbulence in cloud, frequent
6	Severe Turbulence in clear air, infrequent
7	Severe Turbulence in clear air, frequent
8	Severe Turbulence in cloud, infrequent
9	Severe Turbulence in cloud, frequent

TABLE 5 f_c
0	In the clear
8	In and out of clouds
9	In clouds all the time (continuous IMC)
/	Impossible to determine due to darkness or other cause

TABLE 6 d_t
0	Spot of Wind
1	Average wind
/	No wind reported

TABLE 7 d_a
0	Winds obtained using doppler radar or inertial systems
1	Winds obtained using other navigation equipment and/or techniques
/	Navigator unable to determine or wind not compatible

TABLE 8 w
0	Clear
1	Scattered (trace to 4/8 cloud coverage)
2	Broken (5/8 to 7/8 cloud coverage)
3	Overcast/undercast
4	Fog, thick dust or haze
5	Drizzle
6	Rain (continuous or intermittent precip - from stratiform clouds)
7	Snow or rain and snow mixed
8	Shower(s) (continuous or intermittent precip - from cumuliform clouds)
9	Thunderstorm(s)
/	Unknown for any cause, including darkness

TABLE 9 j
0	Sea level pressure in whole millibars (thousands fig if any omitted)
1	Altitude 200 mb surface in geopotential decameters (thousands fig if any omitted)
2	Altitude 850 mb surface in geopotential meters (thousands fig omitted)
3	Altitude 700 mb surface in geopotential meters (thousands fig omitted)
4	Altitude 500 mb surface in geopotential decameters
5	Altitude 400 mb surface in geopotential decameters
6	Altitude 300 mb surface in geopotential decameters
7	Altitude 250 mb surface in geopotential decameters (thousands fig if any omitted)
8	D - Value in geopotential decameters; if negative 500 is added to HHH
9	Altitude 925 mb surface in geopotential meters
/	No absolute altitude available or geopotential data not within ± 30 meters/4 mb accuracy requirements

TABLE 10 N_s
0	No additional cloud layers (place holder)
1	1 okta or less, but not zero (1/8 or less sky covered)
2	2 oktas (or 2/8 of sky covered)
3	3 oktas (or 3/8 of sky covered)
4	4 oktas (or 4/8 of sky covered)
5	5 oktas (or 5/8 of sky covered)
6	6 oktas (or 6/8 of sky covered)
7	7 oktas or more but not 8 oktas
8	8 oktas or sky completely covered
9	Sky obscured (place holder)

TABLE 11 C
0	Cirrus (Ci)
1	Cirrocumulus (Cc)
2	Cirrostratus (Cs)
3	Altocumulus (Ac)
4	Altostratus (As)
5	Nimbostratus (Ns)
6	Stratocumulus (Sc)
7	Stratus (St)
8	Cumulus (Cu)
9	Cumulonimbus (Cb)
/	Cloud type unknown due to darkness or other analogous phenomena

TABLE 12 $h_s h_s H_t H_t h_i h_i H_i H_i$
00	Less than 100
01	100 ft
02	200 ft
03	300 ft
etc, etc	
49	4,900 ft
50	5,000 ft
51-55	Not used
56	6,000 ft
57	7,000 ft
etc, etc	
79	29,000 ft
80	30,000 ft
81	35,000 ft
82	40,000 ft
etc, etc	
89	Greater than 70,000 ft
//	Unknown

TABLE 13 d_w
0	No report	5	SW
1	NE	6	W
2	E	7	NW
3	SE	8	N
4	S	9	all directions

TABLE 14 W_s
0	No change
1	Marked wind shift
2	Beginning or ending or marked turbulence
3	Marked temperature change (not with altitude)
4	Precipitation begins or ends
5	Change in cloud forms
6	Fog or ice fog bank begins or ends
7	Warm front
8	Cold Front
9	Front, type not specified

TABLE 15 $S_b S_e S_s$
0	No report
1	Previous position
2	Present position
3	30 nautical miles
4	60 nautical miles
5	90 nautical miles
6	120 nautical miles
7	150 nautical miles
8	180 nautical miles
9	More than 180 nautical miles
/	Unknown (not used for S_s)

TABLE 16 w_d

0 No report
1 Signs of a tropical cyclone
2 Ugly threatening sky
3 Duststorm or sandstorm
4 Fog or ice fog
5 Waterspout
6 Cirrostratus shield or bank
7 Altostratus or altocumulus shield or bank
8 Line of heavy cumulus
9 Cumulonimbus heads or thunderstorms

TABLE 17 I_r

7 Light
8 Moderate
9 Severe
/ Unknown or contrails

TABLE 18 I_t

0 None
1 Rime ice in clouds
2 Clear ice in clouds
3 Combination rime and clear ice in clouds
4 Rime ice in precipitation
5 Clear ice in precipitation
6 Combination rime and clear ice in precip
7 Frost (icing in clear air)
8 Nonpersistent contrails (less than 1/4 nautical miles long)
9 Persistent contrails

TABLE 19 S_r, E_w, E_l

0 0NM	5 50NM
1 10NM	6 60-80NM
2 20NM	7 80-100NM
3 30NM	8 100-150NM
4 40NM	9 Greater than 150NM
	/ Unknown

TABLE 20 O_e

0 Circular
1 NNE - SSW
2 NE - SW
3 ENE - WSW
4 E - W
5 ESE - WNW
6 SE - NW
7 SSE - NNW
8 S - N
/ Unknown

TABLE 21 c_e

1 Scattered Area
2 Solid Area
3 Scattered Line
4 Solid Line
5 Scattered, all quadrants
6 Solid, all quadrants
/ Unknown

TABLE 22 i_e

2 Weak
5 Moderate
8 Strong
/ Unknown

TABLE 23 V_i

1 Inflight visibility 0 to and including 1 nautical mile
2 Inflight visibility greater than 1 and not exceeding 3 nautical miles
3 Inflight visibility greater than 3 nautical miles

RECCO SYMBOLIC FORM

SECTION ONE (MANDATORY)

$9XXX9 \ GGggi_d \ YQL_aL_aL_a \ L_oL_oL_oBf_c \ h_ah_ah_ad_td_a$

$ddfff \ TTT_dT_dw \ /jHHH$

SECTION TWO (ADDITIONAL)

$1k_nN_sN_sN_s \ Ch_sh_sH_tH_t \ ..... \ ..... \ 4ddff$

$6W_sS_sW_dd_w \ 7I_rI_tS_bS_e \ 7h_ih_iH_iH_i \ 8d_rd_rS_rO_e$

$8E_wE_lc_ei_e \ 9V_iT_wT_wT_w$

SECTION THREE (INTERMEDIATE)

$9XXX9 \ GGggi_d \ YQL_aL_aL_a \ L_oL_oL_oBf_c \ h_ah_ah_ad_td_a$

$ddfff \ TTT_dT_dw \ /jHHH$

Table G-2. Reconnaissance Code Regulations

1. At the time of the observation the aircraft observing platform is considered to be located on the axis of a right vertical cylinder with a radius of 30 nautical miles bounded by the earth's surface and the top atmosphere. Present weather, cloud amount and type, turbulence, and other subjective elements are reported as occurring within the cylinder. Flight level winds, temperature, dew point, and geopotential values are sensed or computed and reported as occurring at the center of the observation circle. Radar echoes, significant weather changes, distant weather, and icing are phenomena that may also be observed/reported. Code groups identifying these phenomena may be reported as necessary to adequately describe met conditions observed.

2. The intermediate observation (Section Three) is reported following Section One (or Section Two if appended to Section One) in the order that it was taken.

3. Plain language remarks may be added as appropriate. These remarks follow the last encoded portion of the horizontal or vertical observation and will clearly convey the intended message. Vertical observations will not include meteorological remarks. These remarks must begin with a letter or word-e.g. "FL TEMP" vice "700 MB FL TEMP." The last report plain language remarks are mandatory, i.e., "LAST REPORT. OBS 01 thru 08 to KNHC, OBS 09 and 10 to KBIX."

4. The hundreds digit of longitude is omitted for longitudes from 100° to 180°.

5. Describe conditions along the route of flight actually experienced at flight level by aircraft.

6. TT, T_dT_d. When encoding negative temperatures, 50 is added to the absolute value of the temperature with the hundreds figure, if any, being omitted. A temperature of -52°C is encoded as 02, the distinction between -52°C and 2°C being made from i_d. Missing or unknown temperatures are reported as //. When the dew point is colder than -49.4°C, Code T_dT_d as // and report the actual value as a plain language remark - e.g. "DEW POINT NEG 52°C".

7. When two or more types of w co-exist, the type with the higher code figure will be reported. Code Figure 1, 2 and 3 are reported based on the total cloud amount through a given altitude, above or below the aircraft, and when other figures are inappropriate. The summation principle applies only when two or more cloud types share a given altitude.

8. When j is reported as a /, HHH is encoded as ///.

9. If the number of cloud layers reported exceeds 3, k_n in the first 1-group reports the total number of cloud layers. The second 1-group reports the additional number of layers being reported exclusive of those previously reported. In those cases where a cloud layer(s) is discernible, but a descriptive cloud picture of the observation circle is not possible, use appropriate remarks such as "Clouds Blo" or "As Blo" to indicate the presence of clouds. In such cases, coded entries are not made for group 9. The sequence in which cloud amounts are encoded depends upon type of cloud, cloud base, and vertical extent of the cloud. The cloud with the largest numerical value of cloud type code (C) is reported first, regardless of coverage, base, or vertical extent. Among clouds of the same cloud type code, sharing a common base, the cloud of greatest vertical extent is reported first. The summation principle is not used; each layer is treated as though no other clouds were present. The total amount of clouds through one altitude shared by several clouds will not exceed 8 oktas. Only use code figure 0 as a place holder when you can determine that no additional cloud layers exist. In case of undercast, overcast, etc., use code figure 9 as a placeholder.

10. Due to limitations in the ability to distinguish sea state features representative of wind speeds above 130 knots, surface wind speeds in excess of 130 knots will not be encoded. Wind speeds of 100 to 130 knots inclusive will be encoded by deleting the hundreds figure and adding 50 to dd. For wind speeds above 130 knots, dd is reported without adding 50 and ff is encoded as // with a plain language remark added, i.e., "SFC WIND ABOVE 130 KNOTS."

11. Significant weather changes which have occurred since the last observation along the track are reported for W_s.

12. When aircraft encounters icing in level flight, the height at which the icing occurred will be reported for h_ih_i. The H_iH_i will be reported as //.

THE HDOB MESSAGE

The HDOB message is used to transmit High-Density/High-Accuracy (HD/HA) meteorological data from hurricane reconnaissance aircraft. These are created automatically by the system software. Each message consists of a communications header line (Table G-3), a mission/ob identifier line (Table G-4), and 20 lines of HD/HA data (Table G-5).

Within an HDOB message, the time interval (resolution) between individual HD/HA observations can be set by the operator to be 30, 60, or 120 seconds. However, regardless of the time resolution of the HD/HA data, the meteorological parameters in the HDOB message always represent 30-second averages along the flight track (except for certain peak values as noted in Table G-5).

The nominal time of each HD/HA record is the midpoint of the 30-second averaging interval. This means that an HD/HA record at time t will include data measured at time t+15 seconds. For purposes of determining peak flight-level and SFMR winds, the encoding interval begins 15 seconds after the nominal time of the last HD/HA record and ends 15 seconds after the nominal time of the record being encoded.

A sample HDOB message is given below (message begins with URNT15...):

```
0         1         2         3         4         5         6         7
01234567890123456789012345678901234567890123456789012345678901234567890
-----------------------------------------------------------------------

URNT15 KNHC 281426
AF302 1712A KATRINA            HDOB 41 20050928
142030 2608N 08756W 7093 03047 9333 +192 +134 133083 089 080 /// 00
142100 2609N 08755W 7091 03054 9330 +166 +146 133106 115 103 /// 00
142130 2610N 08754W 7058 03040 9295 +134 +134 135121 124 111 /// 00
142200 2611N 08753W 7037 03060 9291 +124 +124 138129 136 122 /// 00
 .
 .
 .
142230 2612N 08752W 7010 03057 9282 +102 +102 141153 166 148 /// 00
142300 2612N 08751W 7042 03010 9293 +088 +083 133159 164 147 /// 00
142330 2613N 08750W 6999 03064 9279 +088 +088 138158 161 144 /// 00
142400 2614N 08749W 7005 03046 9281 +080 +080 138155 158 142 /// 00
142430 2614N 08748W 6998 03048 9278 +078 +078 138151 153 137 /// 00
142500 2615N 08747W 7002 03048 9279 +084 +084 140146 148 133 /// 00
$$
```

Figure G-2. HDOB Description and Sample Message

Table G-3. Communications Headers for HDOB Messages

NODE	AWIPS ID	WMO HEADER	OCEAN BASIN
MIA	AHONT1	URNT15	Atlantic
MIA	AHOPN1	URPN15	East and Central Pacific
MIA	AHOPA1	URPA15	West Pacific

Table G-4. Mission/Ob Identifier Line Format for HDOB Messages

A sample mission/ob identifier line is given below (beginning with AF302...), followed by a description of the parameters.

```
0         1         2         3         4         5         6         7
0123456789012345678901234567890123456789012345678901234567890123456789 0
-------------------------------------------------------------------------
IIIIIIIIIIIIIIIIIIIIIIIIIIIIIIIIIII HDOB NN YYYYMMDD

AF302 1712A KATRINA           HDOB 41 20050928   ← example
```

III...III: Mission identifier, as determined in Chapter 5, paragraph 5.7.6.

NN: Observation number (01-99), assigned sequentially for each HDOB message during the flight. This sequencing is independent of the numbering of other types of messages (RECCO, DROP, VORTEX, etc.), which have their own numbering sequence.

YYYYMMDD: Year, month, and day of the first HD/HA data line of the message.

Table G-5. HD/HA Data Line Format for HDOB Messages

```
0         1         2         3         4         5         6         7
01234567890123456789012345678901234567890123456789012345678901234567890
-------------------------------------------------------------------------
hhmmss LLLLH NNNNNW PPPP GGGGG XXXX sTTT sddd wwwSSS MMM KKK ppp FF
142230 2612N 08752W 7010 03057 9282 +102 +102 141153 166 148 /// 00
```

hhmmss: Observation time, in hours, minutes and seconds (UTC). The observation time is the midpoint of the 30-s averaging interval used for the record's meteorological data.

LLLLH: The latitude of the aircraft at the observation time in degrees (LL) and minutes (LL). The hemisphere (H) is given as either N or S.

NNNNNH: The longitude of the aircraft at the observation time, in degrees (NNN) and minutes (NN). The hemisphere (H) is given as either E or W.

PPPP: Aircraft static air pressure, in tenths of mb with decimal omitted, at the observation time. If pressure is equal to or greater than 1000 mb the leading 1 is dropped.

GGGGG: Aircraft geopotential height, in meters, at the observation time.

XXXX: Extrapolated surface pressure or D-value (30-s average). Encoded as extrapolated surface pressure if aircraft static pressure is 550.0 mb or greater (i.e., flight altitudes at or below 550 mb). Format for extrapolated surface pressure is the same as for static pressure. For flight altitudes higher than 550 mb, **XXXX** is encoded as the D-value, in meters. Negative D-values are encoded by adding 5000 to the D-value. /// indicates missing value.

s: Sign of the temperature or dew point (+ or -).

sTTT: The air temperature in degrees and tenths Celsius, decimal omitted (30-s average). /// indicates missing value.

sddd: The dew point temperature, in degrees and tenths Celsius, decimal omitted (30-s average). /// indicates missing value.

www: Wind direction in degrees (30-s average). North winds are coded as 000. /// indicates missing value.

SSS: Wind speed, in kt (30-s average). /// indicates missing value.

MMM: Peak 10-second average wind speed occurring within the encoding interval, in kt.

/// indicates missing value.

KKK: Peak 10-second average surface wind speed occurring within the encoding interval from the Stepped Frequency Microwave Radiometer (SFMR), in kt. /// indicates missing value.

ppp: SFMR-derived rain rate, in mm hr^{-1}, evaluated over the 10-s interval chosen for KKK . /// indicates missing value.

FF: Quality control flags.

First column indicates status of positional variables as follows:
0 All parameters of nominal accuracy
1 Lat/lon questionable
2 Geopotential altitude or static pressure questionable
3 Both lat/lon and GA/PS questionable

Second column indicates status of meteorological variables as follows:
0 All parameters of nominal accuracy
1 T or TD questionable
2 Flight-level winds questionable
3 SFMR parameter(s) questionable
4 T/TD and FL winds questionable
5 T/TD and SFMR questionable
6 FL winds and SFMR questionable
9 T/TD, FL winds, and SFMR questionable

Table G-6. TEMP DROP CODE

EXTRACT FROM: WMO-No. 306 MANUAL ON CODES
FM 37-X Ext. TEMP DROP: Upper-level pressure, temperature, humidity and wind report from a sonde released by carrier balloons or aircraft. See Figure G-3 for an example TEMP DROP message for tropical cyclone operations.

CODE FORM:

PART A

SECTION 1 $M_iM_iM_jM_j$ $YYGGI_d$ $99L_aL_aL_a$ $Q_cL_oL_oL_oL_o$ $MMMU_{La}U_{Lo}$

SECTION 2 $99P_oP_oP_o$ $T_oT_oT_{ao}D_oD_o$ $d_od_of_of_of_o$

                  $P_1P_1h_1h_1h_1$ $T_1T_1T_{a1}D_1D_1$ $d_1d_1f_1f_1f_1$

                  $P_nP_nh_nh_nh_n$ $T_nT_nT_{an}D_nD_n$ $d_nd_nf_nf_nf_n$

SECTION 3 $88P_tP_tP_t$ $T_tT_tT_{at}D_tD_t$ $d_td_tf_tf_tf_t$
            or
            88999

SECTION 4 $77P_mP_mP_m$ $d_md_mf_mf_mf_m$ $(4v_bv_bv_av_a)$
            or
            $66P_mP_mP_m$ $d_md_mf_mf_mf_m$ $(4v_bv_bv_av_a)$
            or
            77999

SECTION 10   31313

             51515 $101A_{df}A_{df}$ $0P_nP_nP'_nP'_n.$
                     or
                     $101A_{df}A_{df}$ $P_nP_nh_nh_nh_n$
             61616

             62626

PART B

SECTION 1 $M_iM_iM_jM_j$ $YYGG8$ $99L_aL_aL_a$ $Q_cL_oL_oL_o$ $MMMU_{La}U_{Lo}$

SECTION 5 $n_on_oP_oP_oP_o$ $T_oT_oT_{ao}D_oD_o$

                  $n_1n_1P_1P_1P_1$ $T_1T_1T_{a1}D_1D_1$

                  $n_nn_nP_nP_nP_n$ $T_nT_nT_{an}D_nD_n$

SECTION 6   21212 $n_on_oP_oP_oP_o$ $d_od_of_of_of_o$

$$n_1n_1P_1P_1P_1 \quad d_1d_1f_1f_1f_1$$

$$n_nn_nP_nP_nP_n \quad d_nd_nf_nf_nf_n$$

SECTION 7	31313	$s_rr_ar_as_as_a$	8GGgg
SECTION 9	51515	$101A_{df}A_{df}$	or
	$101A_{df}A_{df}$	$0P_nP_nP'_nP'_n$.	or
	$101A_{df}A_{df}$	$P_nP_nh_nh_nh_n$	
SECTION 10	61616		
	62626		

PART ALPHA (A)

IDENTIFICATION LETTERS: M_JM_J

Identifier: M_JM_J - Identifier for Part A of the report.

DATE/TIME GROUP: $YYGGI_d$

Identifier: **YY** - Date group
Identifier: **GG** - Time group
Identifier: I_d - The highest mandatory level for which wind is available.

LATTITUDE: $99L_aL_aL_a$

Identifier: **99** – Indicator for data on position follows.
Identifier: $L_aL_aL_a$ – Latitude in tenths of degrees

LONGITUDE: $Q_cL_oL_oL_oL_o$

Identifier: Q_c – The octant of the globe.
Identifier: $L_oL_oL_oL_o$ – Longitude in tenths of degrees

MARSDEN SQUARE: $MMMU_{la}U_{lo}$

Identifier: **MMM** - Marsden square.
Identifier: $U_{la}U_{lo}$ – Units digits in the reported latitude and longitude.

SEA LEVEL PRESSURE: $99P_0P_0P_0 \quad T_0T_0T_0D_0D_0 \quad d_0d_0f_0f_0f_0$

Identifier: **99** – Indicator for data at the surface level follows
Identifier: $P_0P_0P_0$ – Indicator for pressure of specified levels in whole millibars (thousands digit omitted)
Identifier: $T_0T_0T_0$ – Tens and digits of air temperature (not rounded off) in degrees Celsius, at specified levels beginning with surfacc.
Identifier: D_0D_0 – Dewpoint depression at standard isobaric surfaces beginning with surface level.

NOTE
When the depression is 4.9C or less encode the units and tenths digits of the depression. Encode depressions of 5.0 through 5.4C as 50. Encode depressions of 5.5C through 5.9C as 56. Dew point

depressions of 6.0 and above are encoded in tens and units with 50 added. Dew point depressions for relative humidities less then 20% are encoded as 80. When air temperature is below –40C report D_nD_n as //.

Identifier: d_od_o – True direction from which wind is blowing rounded to nearest 5 degrees. Report hundreds and tens digits. The unit digit (0 or 5) is added to the hundreds digit of wind speed.

Identifier: $f_of_of_o$ – Wind speed in knots. Hundreds digit is sum of speed and unit digit of direction, i.e. 29$\underline{5}$° at 125 knots encoded as 29$\underline{6}$25.

NOTE: 1. When flight level is just above a standard surface and in the operator's best meteorological judgment, the winds are representative of the winds at the standard surface, then the operator may encode the standard surface winds using the data from flight level. If the winds are not representative, then encode /////.

NOTE: 2. The wind group relating to the surface level ($d_od_of_of_o$) will be included in the report; when the corresponding wind data are not available, the group will be encoded as /////.

STANDARD ISOBARIC SURFACES : $P_1P_1h_1h_1h_1$ $T_1T_1T_1D_1D_1$ $d_1d_1f_1f_1f_1$

Identifier: P_1P_1 – Pressure of standard isobaric surfaces in units of tens of millibars.
  (1000 mbs = 00, 925mbs = 92, 850mbs = 85, 700mbs = 70, 500mbs = 50, 400mbs = 40, 300mbs = 30, 250mbs = 25).
Identifier: $h_1h_1h_1$ – Heights of the standard pressure level in geopotential meters or decameters above the surface. Encoded in decameters at and above 500mbs omitting, if necessary, the thousands or tens of thousands digits. Add 500 to hhh for negative 1000mb or 925mb heights. Report 1000mb group as 00/// ///// ///// when pressure is less than 950mbs.
Identifier: $T_1T_1T_1D_1D_1$ – Same temperature/dew point encoding procedures apply to all levels.
Identifier : $d_1d_1f_1f_1f_1$ – Same wind encoding procedures apply to all levels.

DATA FOR TROPOPAUSE LEVELS: 88 $P_tP_tP_t$ $T_tT_tT_tD_tD_t$ $d_td_tf_tf_tf_t$

Identifier: 88 – Indicator for Tropopause level follows
Identifier: $P_tP_tP_t$– Pressure at the tropopause level reported in whole millibars. Report $88P_nP_nP_n$ as 88999 when tropopause is not observed.
Identifier: $T_tT_tT_tD_tD_t$ – Same temperature/ dew point encoding procedures apply.
Identifier: $d_td_tf_tf_tf_t$ - Same wind encoding procedures apply.

MAXIMUM WIND DATA: 77$P_nP_nP_n$ $d_nd_nf_nf_nf_n$ $4v_bv_bv_av_a$

Identifier: 77 – Indicator that data for maximum wind level and for vertical wind shear follow when max wind does not coincide at flight. If the maximum wind level coincides with flight level encode as 66
Identifier: $P_nP_nP_n$ – Pressure at maximum wind level in whole millibars.
Identifier: $d_nd_nf_nf_nf_n$ - Same wind encoding procedures apply.

VERTICAL WIND SHEAR DATA: $4v_bv_bv_av_a$

Identifier: 4 – Data for vertical wind shear follow.
Identifier: v_bv_b – Absolute value of vector difference between max wind and wind 3000 feet BELOW the level of max wind, reported to the nearest knot. Use "//" if missing and a 4 is reported. A vector difference of 99 knots or more is reported with the code figure "99".

Identifier: $v_a v_a$ – Absolute value of vector difference between max wind and wind 3000 feet above the level of max wind, reported to the nearest knot. Use "//" if missing and a 4 is reported. A vector difference of 99 knots or more is reported with the code figure "99".

SOUNDING SYSTEM INDICATION, RADIOSONDE/ SYSTEM STATUS, LAUNCH TIME: 31313 $s_r r_a r_a s_a s_a$ 8GGgg

Identifier: $s_r r_a r_a s_a s_a$ - Sounding system indicator, radiosonde/ system status: $s_a r_a r_a s_a s_a$
Identifier: s_a - Solar and infrared radiation correction (0 – no correction)
Identifier: $r_a r_a$ – Radiosonde/sounding system used (96 – Descending radiosonde)
Identifier: $s_a s_a$ – Tracking technique/status of system used (08 – Automatic satellite navigation)
Identifier: 8GGgg – Launch time
Identifier: 8 – Indicator group
Identifier: GG – Time in hours
Identifier: gg – Time in minutes

ADDITIONAL DATA GROUPS: 51515 101XX $0P_n P_n P_n P_n$

Identifier: 51515 – Additional data in regional code follow
Identifier: 10166 – Geopotential data are doubtful between the following levels $0P_n P_n P_n P_n$. This code figure is used only when geopotential data are doubtful from one level to another.
Identifier: 10167 – Temperature data are doubtful between the following levels $0P_n P_n P_n P_n$. This code figure shall be reported when only the temperature data are doubtful for a portion of the descent. If a 10167 group is reported a 10166 will also be reported. EXAMPLE: Temperature is doubtful from 540mbs to 510mbs. SLP is 1020mbs. The additional data groups would be : 51515 10166 00251 10167 05451.
Identifier: 10190 – Extrapolated altitude data follows:

When the sounding begins within 25mbs below a standard surface, the height of the surface is reported in the format 10190 $P_n P_n h_n h_n h_n$ The temperature group is not reported. EXAMPLE: Assume the release was made from 310mbs and the 300mb height was 966 decameters. The last reported standard level in Part A is the 400mb level. The data for the 300mb level is reported in Part A and B as 1019030966.

When the sounding does not reach surface, but terminates within 25mbs of a standard surface, the height of the standard surface is reported in Part A of the code in standard format and also at the end of Part A and Part B of the code in the format as 10190 $P_n P_n h_n h_n h_n$.
EXAMPLE: Assume termination occurred at 980mbs and the extrapolated height of the 1000mb level was 115 meters. The 1000mb level would be reported in Part A of the code as 00115 ///// ///// and in Part B as 10190 00115.

Identifier: 10191 – Extrapolated surface pressure precedes. Extrapolated surface pressure is only reported when the termination occurs between 850mbs and the surface. Surface pressure is reported in Part A as 99$P_0 P_0 P_0$ ///// and in Part B as 00$P_0 P_0 P_0$ /////. When surface pressure is extrapolated the 10191 group is the last additional data group reported in Part B.

AIRCRAFT AND MISSION IDENTIFICATION: 61616 AFXXX XXXXX XXXXX OB X

Identifier: 61616 – Aircraft and mission identification data follows.
Identifier: AFXXX – The identifier AF for U.S. Air Force and the last three digits of the aircraft's tail number.
Identifier: XXXXX XXXXX – The identifier for the type of mission being flown.

If a training mission the mission identifier is WXWXA TRAIN. The fifth letter "A" is the only character that could possibly change. The "A" indicates that the flight originated in the Atlantic basin. The letter "C" identifies the Central Pacific area, and the letter "E" identifies the Eastern Pacific.

If an operational storm mission: the first two numbers Identifier the number of times an aircraft has flown this system and the second two numbers Identifier the system number. The last character

again identifies the basin flown. The name of the storm would replace TRAIN.
EXAMPLE: AF968 0204A MARIE – Aircraft number 50968, this was the second flight into this system and the system was the fourth of the season. The system reached tropical storm strength and was named MARIE.

Identifier: **OB 14** – The observation (both vertical and horizontal) number as transmitted from the aircraft.

NATIONALLY DEVELOPED CODES: 62626

Identifier: **62626** – This is the remarks section. Only the remarks EYE, EYEWALL XXX, MXWNDBND, or RAINBAND will be used. If the remark EYEWALL is used it will be followed by the octant (degrees) sonde is located relative to eye center. Example: If the sonde is released in the NE quad of the storm, XXX is 045.

Identifier: **REL XXXXNXXXXW hhmmss** - the time and location of the highest (in altitude) wind reported in the temp drop message

Identifier: **SPG XXXXNXXXXW hhmmss** - the time and location of the lowest (in altitude) wind reported in the temp drop message.

Identifier: **SPL XXXXNXXXXW hhmm** - Impact location of the sonde based on its last GPS position and the splash time. (SPL has less precision than SPG and may be removed in the next version of the NHOP).

Identifier: **LAST WND XXX** - Height of the last reported wind. If a surface wind is reported the Last Wind remark is omitted. XXX will never be less than 13 meters

Identifier: **MBL WND dddff** - The mean boundary level wind. The mean wind in the lowest 500 meters of the sounding

Identifier: **AEV XXXXX** - This is the software version being used for the sounding.

Identifier: **DLM WND ddfff bbbttt** - The Deep Layer Mean wind. It is the average wind over the depth of the sounding. Where ddfff is the wind averaged from the first to the last available wind (these would correspond to the first and last significant levels for wind); ttt is the pressure at the top of the layer, and bbb is the pressure at the bottom of the layer (in whole mbs, with thousands digit omitted).

Identifier: **WL150 ddfff zzz** - Average wind over the lowest available 150 m of the wind sounding. Where ddfff is the mean wind over the 150 m layer centered at zzz m.

PART ALPHA (B)

DATA FOR SIGNIFICANT TEMPERATURE AND RELATIVE HUMIDITY LEVELSSIGNIFICANT ISOBARIC LEVELS:
$n_0n_0P_0P_0P_0$ $T_0T_0T_0D_0D_0$

IDENTIFICATION LETTERS: M_JM_J

Identifier: M_JM_J - Identifier for Part B of the report.

DATE/TIME GROUP: YYGG8

Identifier: **YY** - Date group
Identifier: **GG** - Time group
Identifier: **8** - Indicator for the use of satellite navigation for windfinding.

LATTITUDE: $99L_aL_aL_a$ (Same as Part A)

LONGITUDE: $Q_cL_oL_oL_oL_o$ (Same as Part A)

MARSDEN SQUARE: $MMMU_{la}U_{lo}$ (Same as Part A)
SEA LEVEL PRESSURE: $n_0n_0P_0P_0P_0$ $T_0T_0T_0D_0D_0$

Identifier: **nono** – Indicator for number of level starting with surface level. Only surface will be numbered as "00".
Identifier: $P_0P_0P_0$ – Indicator for pressure of specified levels in whole millibars (thousands digit omitted)
Identifier: $T_0T_0T_0$ – Tens and digits of air temperature (not rounded off) in degrees Celsius, at specified levels beginning with surface.

Identifier: D_0D_0 – Dewpoint depression at standard isobaric surfaces beginning with surface level. Encoded the same as Part A.

FOR STORM DROPS ONLY. If SLP is less than 950mb encode the 1000mb group as 00/// ///// //////. When the SLP is between 950mb and 999mb encode 1000mb as 00PoPoPo ///// ///// (500 meters are added to height below surface).

DATA FOR SIGNIFICANT WIND LEVELS: $n_0n_0P_0P_0P_0 \ d_0d_0f_0f_0f_0$

Identifier: n_0n_0 – Number of level starting with surface level. Only surface will be numbered as **"00"**.
Identifier: $P_0P_0P_0$ – Pressure at specified levels in whole millibars.
Identifier: d_0d_0 – True direction from which wind is blowing rounded to nearest 5 degrees. Report hundreds and tens digits. The unit digit (0 or 5) is added to the hundreds digit of wind speed.
Identifier: $f_0f_0f_0$ – Wind speed in knots. Hundreds digit is sum of speed and unit digit of direction, i.e. 295° at 125 knots encoded as 29625.

Same notes in Part A apply.

31313, 51515, 61616, 62626 – Repeated from Part A.

FIGURE G-3. EXAMPLE TEMP DROP MESSAGE FOR TROPICAL CYCLONES

UZNT13 KNHC 080839
XXAA 58088 99192 70803 04590 99964 21676 20581 00814 ///// //////
92359 20476 22611 85085 18876 24614 88999 77999
31313 09608 80747
51515 10190 70752
61616 AF302 0617A PALOMA   OB 16
62626 EYEWALL 225 SPL 1925N08021W 0750 MBL WND 22112 AEV 20800 DL
M WND 23107 964833 WL150 21611 079 REL 1920N08030W 074700 SPG 192
6N08021W 075012 =
XXBB 58088 99192 70803 04590 00964 21676 11850 18876 22811 18476
33760 19677 44739 21077 55719 23261 66701 11430
21212 00964 20581 11963 20585 22960 20604 33958 21120 44955 21626
55949 22107 66939 22621 77933 22614 88917 22611 99900 23099 11874
23604 22867 24098 33864 24100 44859 24117 55850 24614 66701 26123
31313 09608 80747
51515 10190 70752
61616 AF302 0617A PALOMA   OB 16
62626 EYEWALL 225 SPL 1925N08021W 0750 MBL WND 22112 AEV 20800 DL
M WND 23107 964833 WL150 21611 079 REL 1920N08030W 074700 SPG 192
6N08021W 075012 =

APPENDIX H

WSR-88D OPERATIONS PLAN FOR TROPICAL CYCLONE EVENTS

To perform radar center-fixing and obtain other diagnostic information, NHC must obtain radar products from WSR-88D sites in the area of landfall. As a tropical cyclone approaches, software commands must be issued at the site, using the Unit Control Position (UCP), in order for NHC to obtain the necessary products. To facilitate this process, NHC, in cooperation with the NWS Weather Forecast Office, Melbourne, and the NEXRAD Radar Operations Center (ROC), has developed an operations plan for use during tropical cyclone events.

The latest edition can be found on the OFCM web site at:
http://www.ofcm.gov/homepage/text/pubs.htm

APPENDIX I

TELEPHONE LISTING

AGENCY	LOCATION	TELEPHONE
Department of Commerce		
NHC Director Atlantic Forecast Operations Pacific Forecast Operations Admin Admin Fax TAFB Lead Forecaster	Miami, FL	COM 305-229-4402 COM 305-229-4415 COM 305-229-4417 COM 305-229-4470 FAX 305-553-1901 COM 305-229-4425
CPHC Director Forecaster and Warning Desk Admin Operations Satellite Coordinator	Honolulu, HI	COM 808-973-5272 COM 808-973-5284 COM 808-973-5270 FAX 808-973-5281 COM 808-973-5285
NOAA Aircraft Operations Center	MacDill AFB, FL	COM 813-828-3310
NCEP/NCO Senior Duty Met (Data QC)	College Park, MD	COM 301-763-8298
Weather Prediction Center (NCEP/WPC)	College Park, MD	COM 301-763-8201
NESDIS Satellite Analysis Branch	College Park, MD	COM 301-763-8444
WFO Guam	Tiyan, Guam	COM 671-472-0950/1/2
NDBC - Operations Branch	Stennis Space Center, MS	COM 228-688-7720
NWS Hydrometeorological Services Core (Headquarters)	Silver Spring, MD	COM 301-713-1858, ext. 108 FAX 301-713-1520
Interdepartmental		
OFCM	Silver Spring, MD	COM 301-427-2002 DSN 851-1460
Department of Defense		
JTWC (Typhoon Duty Officer)	Pearl Harbor, HI	COM 808-474-2320
53rd Weather Reconnaissance Squadron (WRS) Supervisor of Flights Chief ARWO Alternate CARCAH	53 WRS 817 H Street, Suite 201 Keesler AFB, MS 39534-2453	DSN 597-2409 COM 228-377-2409 DSN 597-3207 COM 228-377-3207 DSN 597-9060 COM 228-377-9060
CARCAH OLA, 53d WRS	Miami, FL	COM 305-229-4474 DSN 434-3420
Keesler AFB Command Post	Keesler AFB, MS	COM 228-377-4181/4330 DSN 597-4181/4330
AFWA	Offutt AFB, NE	COM 402-294-2586 DSN 271-2586
FACSFAC VACAPES OAC	Oceana, VA	COM 804-433-1233 DSN 433-1233
17 OWS/WXJ (Satellite Analyst)	Pearl Harbor, HI	COM 787-865-7007 DSN 471-3533
601 AOC/CODW	Tyndall AFB, FL	COM 850-283-5119 DSN 523-5119
Fleet Weather Center	Norfolk, VA	COM 757-444-7583/7750 DSN 564-7583/7750
Fleet Numerical Meteorology & Oceanography Center (FNMOC) (Alternate JTWC)	Monterey, CA	COM 831-656-4325 DSN 878-4325

TMC – Traffic Management Coordinator
OMIC - Operations Manager in Charge

Department of Transportation/Federal Aviation Administration					
Air Route Traffic Control Center (ARTCC)					
ARTCC	Facility ID	Primary Operations Contact Point	Secondary Operations Contact Point (24 hour number)	Operations Fax Number	Center Weather Service Unit (CWSU)
ANCHORAGE	ZAN	907-269-1103 (OMIC)	907-269-1108 (TMC)	907-269-1343	907-269-1145
BOSTON	ZBW	603-879-6663 (TMC)	603-879-6655 (OMIC)	603-879-6461	603-879-6698
HOUSTON	ZHU	281-230-5563 (Missions)	281-230-5560 (OMIC)	281-230-5561	281-230-5676
JACKSONVILLE	ZJX	904-549-1542 (Missions)	904-549-1537 (OMIC)	904-549-1843	904-549-1840 or 904-549-1839
LOS ANGELES	ZLA	661-265-8287 (Missions)	661-265-8205 (OMIC)	661-265-8277	661-265-8258
MIAMI	ZMA	305-716-1589 (Missions)	305-716-1588 (OMIC)	305-716-1511 or 305-716-1577	305-716-1635
NEW YORK	ZNY	631-468-1427 (Missions)	631-468-1080 (STMC)	631-468-4224	631-468-1082
OAKLAND	ZOA	510-745-3332 (Missions)	510-745-3331 (OMIC)	510-745-3339	510-745-3425
SEATTLE	ZSE	253-351-3523 (Missions)	253-351-3520 (OMIC)	253-351-3594 or 253-351-3538	253-351-3741
WASHINGTON	ZDC	703-771-3473 (Missions)	703-771-3470 (OMIC)	703-771-3444	703-771-3480
HONOLULU HCF	ZHN	808-840-6204 (TMC)	808-840-6201 (Front Line Manager)	808-840-6210	N/A
SAN JUAN CERAP	ZSU	787-253-8665 (Front Line Manager)	787-253-8664 (Front Line Manager)	787-253-8650	N/A
GUAM CERAP	ZUA	671-473-1210 (Front Line Manager)	671-473-1270 (Missions)	671-473-1217	N/A

Air Traffic Control System Command Center (ATCSCC)	
MANAGER, ATCSCC	COM 540-422-4004
PRIMARY OPERATIONS CONTACT POINT INTERNATIONAL OPERATIONS POSITION	COM 540-422-4158 FAX 540-422-4196
SECONDARY OPERATIONS CONTACT POINT NATIONAL OPERATIONS MANAGER (NOM)	COM 540-422-4100/4101/4102 800-333-4286 (Military Use Only) FAX 540-422-4196
CENTRAL ALTITUDE RESERVATION FUNCTION (CARF)	COM 540-422-4211/4212 FAX 540-422-4291
US NOTAM Office	COM 540-422-4260/4261 FAX 540-422-4983
DoD Air Traffic Services Cell	COM 540-422-4250 DSN 510-422-4250

STMC – Supervisor Traffic Management Coordinator

Transport Canada (ANS Regulatory Authority)	
Civil Aviation Contingency Operations (CACO) Office	COM (Toll-free from Canada) 1-877-992-6853
	FAX (Toll-free from Canada) 1-866-993-7768

NAV CANADA (ANS Provider)	

National Operations Centre (NOC)	
Admin Hours	0600-2200 (local Eastern time)
NOC (24 Hours) (ATCSCC of Canada)	COM 613-563-5626 COM 613-563-5667 COM (Toll-free from Canada) 1-866-561-9053 COM (Toll-free from U.S.A.) 1-866-651-9056 FAX 613-563-3481
International NOTAM Office (Canada)	COM 613-248-4000 FAX 613-248-4001

Altitude Reservation Units (ARU)	
ARU West (Edmonton ACC) (responsible for Vancouver, Edmonton and Winnipeg FIRs)	COM 780-890-4739 FAX 780-890-4738
ARU East (Gander ACC) (responsible for Toronto, Montreal, Moncton and Gander FIRs)	COM 709-651-5243 FAX 709-651-5288

Area Control Centers (ACC)				
ACC	Facility ID	Primary Operations Contact Point (Shift Manager)	Secondary Operations Contact Point	Fax Number
TORONTO	ZYZ	905-676-4509	905-676-4562	905-612-5613
MONTREAL	ZUL	514-633-3365	514-633-2871	514-633-3371
MONCTON	ZOM	506-867-7173	506-381-4684	506-867-7180
WINNIPEG	ZWG	204-983-8338	204-983-8483	204-984-0030
EDMONTON	ZEG	780-890-8397	780-890-8323	780-890-8011
GANDER	ZQX	709-651-5207	709-651-5223	709-651-5234
VANCOUVER	ZVR	604-598-4500	604-598-4850	604-586-4502

APPENDIX J

GEOGRAPHICAL DEFINING POINTS AND PHONETIC PRONUNCIATIONS

Abaco	AB-a-KO	Escondido	es-cond-dee-dow
Abreojos	aahbray-oh-hoes	Eugenia	ayuh-hen-yuh
Amalie	a-MAHL-ye	Exuma	ek-SOO-ma
Angel	aan-hel		
Anguilla	ang-GWIL-a	Flores	FLO-rish
Antigua	an-TEE-ga	Fort de France	for-de-FRAHCS
Arena	aah-ray-nah		
Arista	ah-ree-staa	Galera	gaa-lehra
Aruba	ah-ROO-ba	Grenada	gre-NAY-dah
Antilles	an-TILL-leez	Guadaloupe	GWAH-deh-loop
Azores	uh-ZOHRZ	Guasave	gwaa-saa-ve
		Guaymas	gwhy-maahs
Bahia	ba-e-yuh		
Ballenas	ba-yaynas	Huatulco	whaa-tool-coe
Barahona	ba-ra-HO-na		
Barbados	bar-BAY-dohz	Islas	eeslas
Barbuda	bar-BOO-dah		
Barra	baa-rra	Jalisco	ha-lee-sco
Barranquilla	Bahr-rahn-KEE-yah	Juanico	whaa-nee-coe
Basse-Terre	baha-TER		
Bimini	BIM-I-ni	Lazaro	laasa-roe
Bonaire	ba-NAIR	Loreto	lo-ae-toe
Burros	bhoorroes	Leeward	LEE-werd
Cap	Haitien kahp ah-ee-SYAN	Manzanillo	manza-nee-oh
Caracas	kah-RAH-kahs	Maracaibo	mar-a-KYE-boh
Cardenas	car-denaass	Maracay	mah-rah-KYE
Caribbean	kar-a-BE-an	Marigot	ma-ree-GOH
Castries	KAS-tree	Mateo	muh-ta-yo
Cayman	kay-MAHN	Mayaguez	may-yah-GWAYS
Champerico	chaam-per-e-coe	Medano	may-daa-no
Charlotte		Melaque	may-laa-kay
Colima	coleema	Merida	MAY-re-thah
Corrientes	cor-re-ehn-tays	Mochis	mo-chees
Cozumel	koh-soo-MEL	Montego	mon-TEE-go
Curacao	koor-a-SOH	Montserrat	mont-se-RAT
Cuyutlan	coo-yootlaan	Mugu	muhgu
		Mulege	moo-lay-hay
Dominica	dom-I-NEE-ka		
Eleuthera	el-OO-thera	Nicaragua	nik-a-RAH-gwah

Ocho Rios	OH-cho REE-os	Tampico	tam-PEE-ko
Oranjestad	o-RAHN-yuh-stat	Tehuantepec	te-whaan-te-pec
		Tela	TAY-lah
Paramaribo	par-a-MAR-I-boh	Tobago	to-BAY-go
Parguera	par-GWER-a	Todos	todohs
Penasco	pen-yaas-co	Tomas	tow-maas
Pointe-a-Pitre	pwan-ta-PEE-tr	Tonala	ton-aahla
Ponce	PON-sa	Tosca	toesca
Port-au-Prince	port-oh-PRINS		
Punta	poonta	Vallarta	vah-yar-ta
Revillagigedo	ray-veeaheehaydo	Yavaros	yaa-vaa-roce
		Yucatan	yoo-ka-TAN
Saba	SAH-ba		
Sao Miguel	soun ME-gel	Zihuatanejo	zeeh-whaa-tanay-
Sipacate	see-paa-caa-tay	ho	
St Croix	ST croy		
St Lucia	ST LOO-she-a		
Soufriere	soo-free-AR		
Surinam	SOOR-I-nam		

APPENDIX K

NHOP OPERATIONAL MAPS
(TERMINAL AREAS)

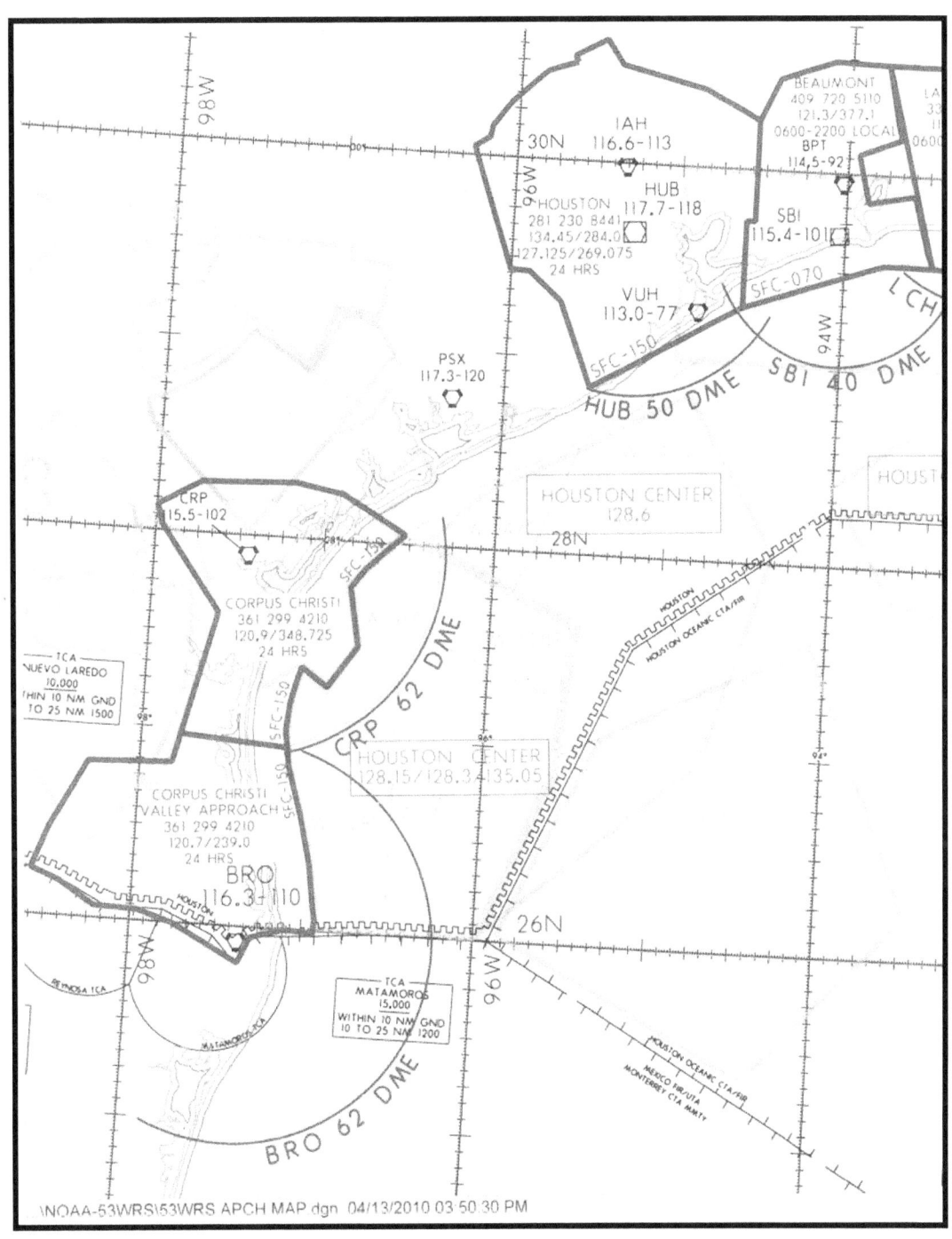

Figure K-1. Texas Coast

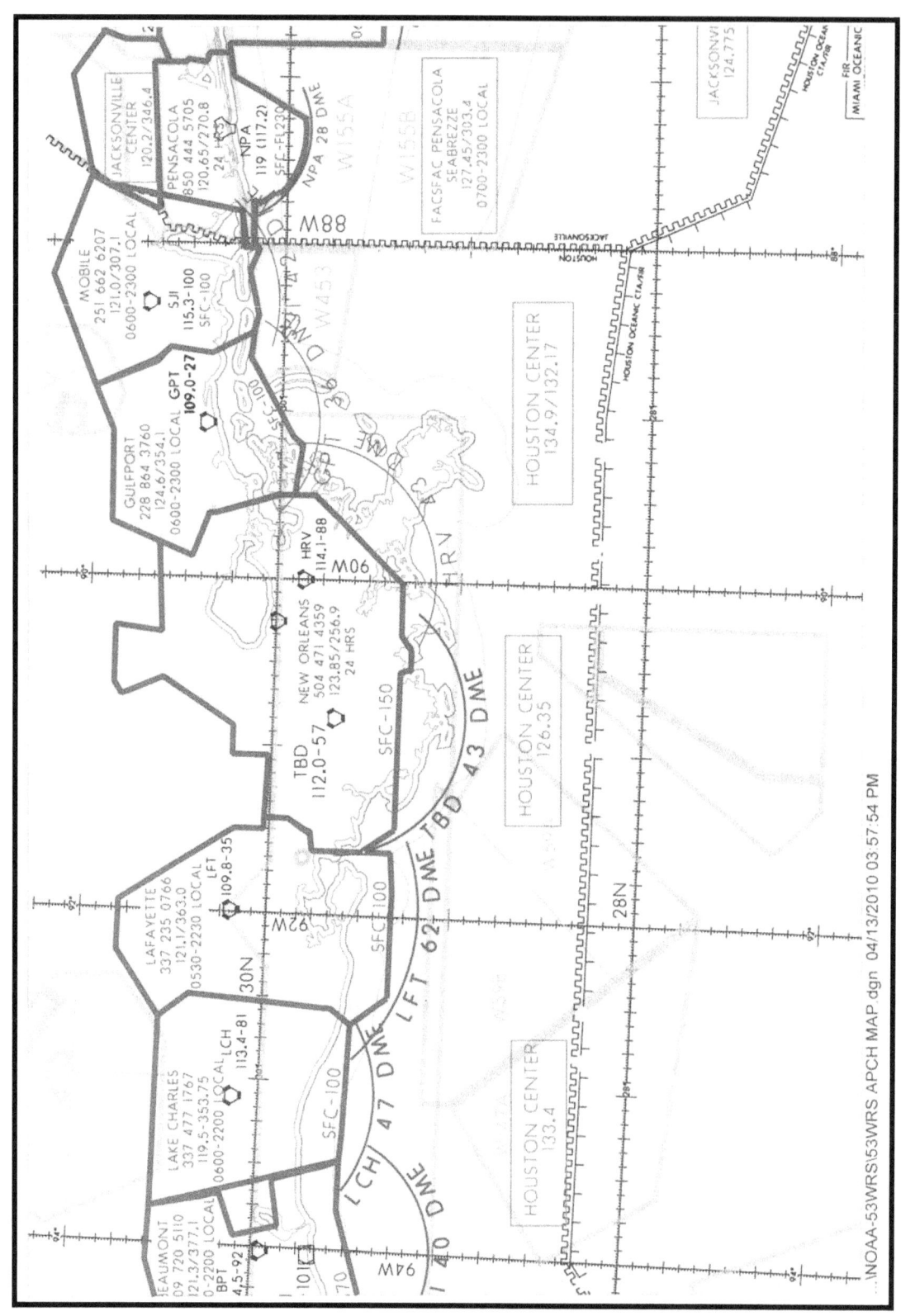

Figure K-2. Lake Charles, LA - Pensacola, FL

K-2

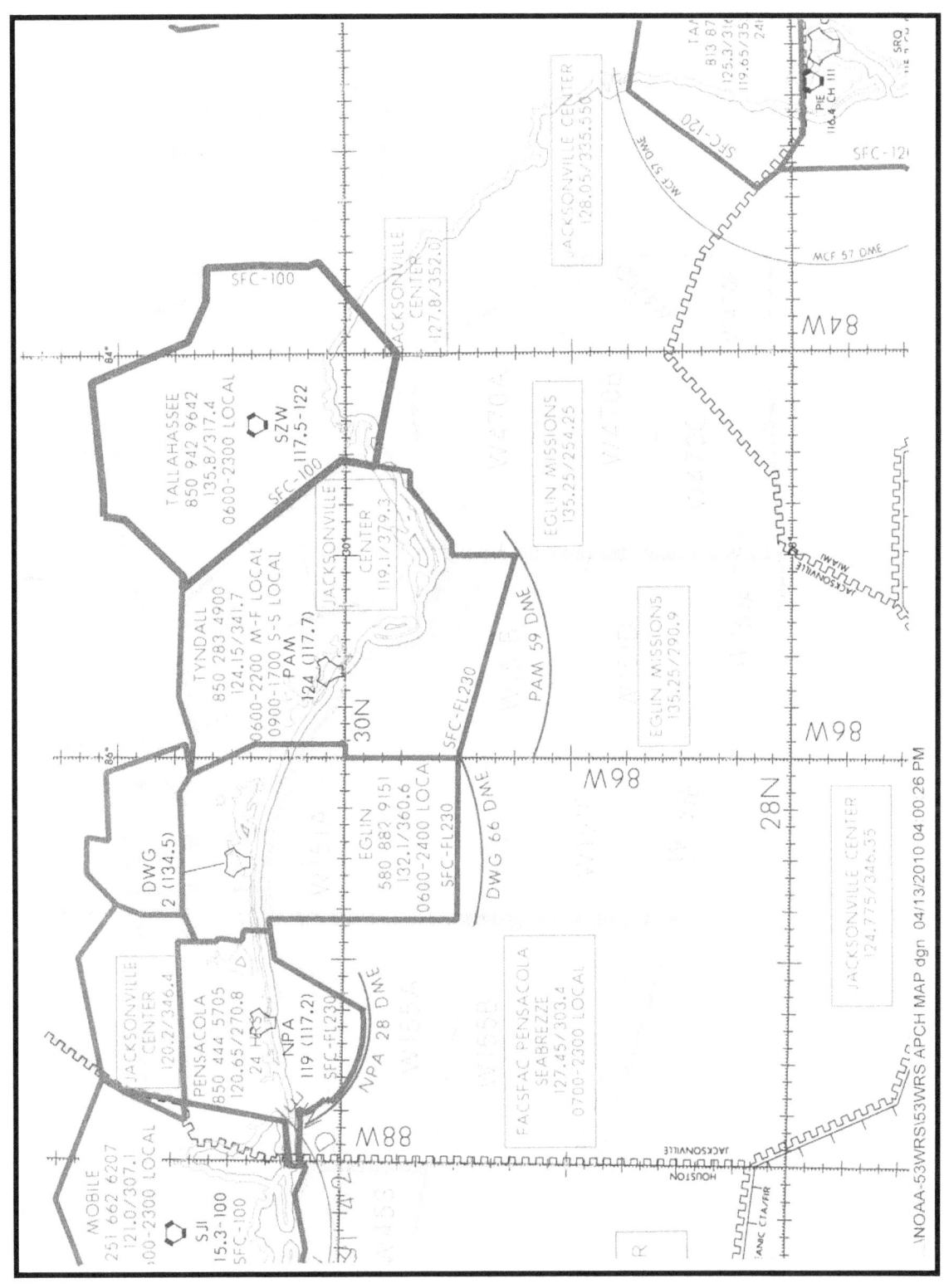

Figure K-3. Pensacola, FL – Tallahassee, FL

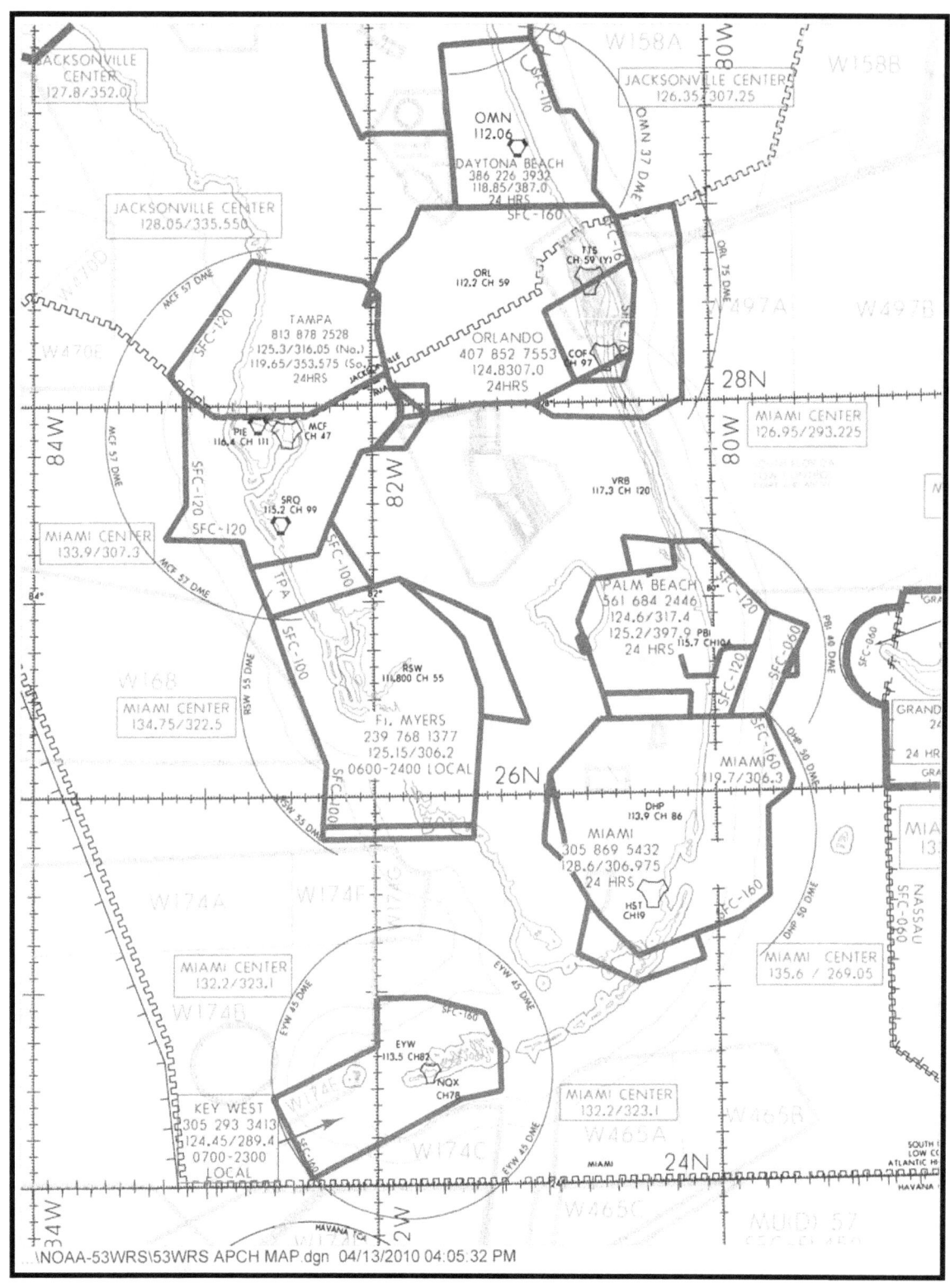

Figure K-4. Central/Southern Florida

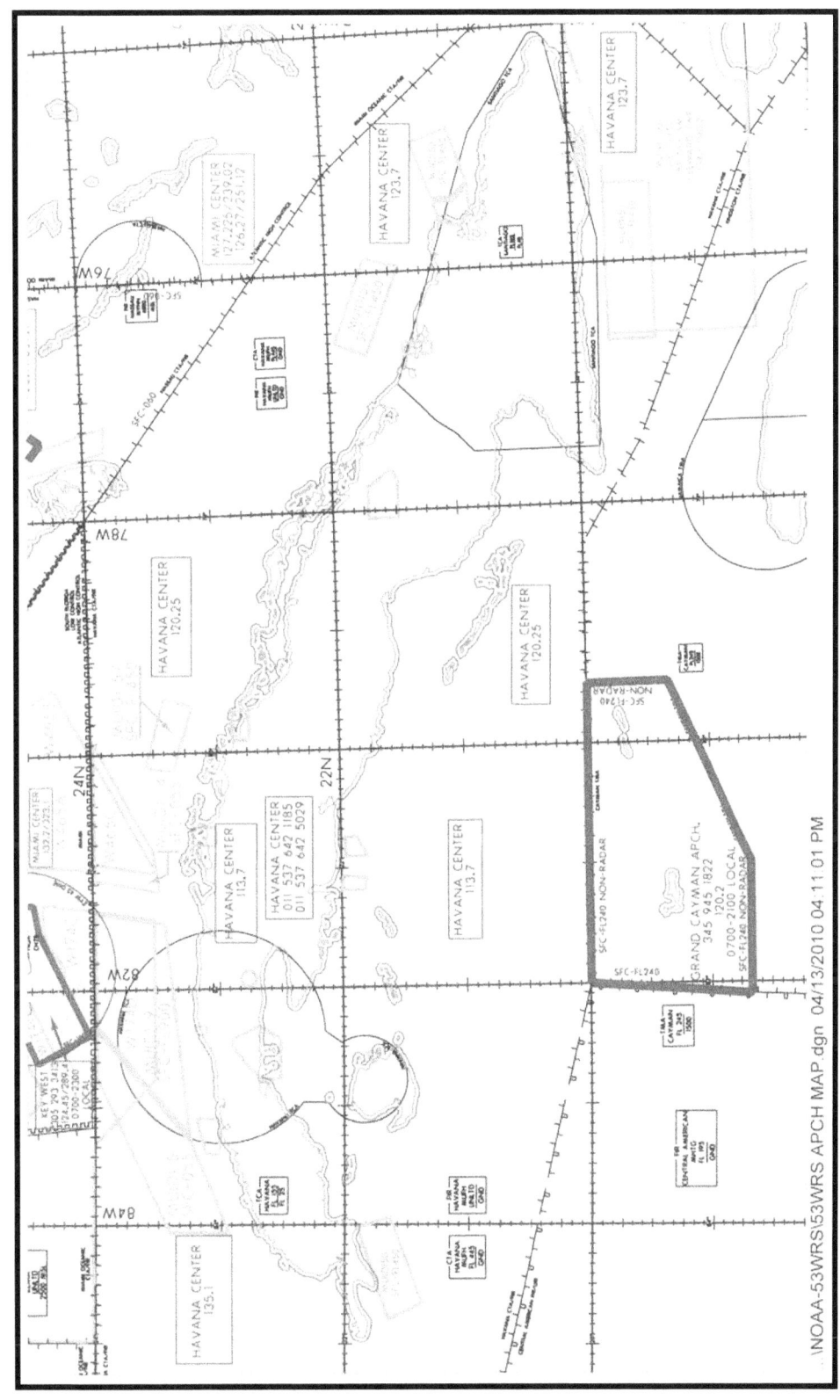

Figure K-5. Cuba – Grand Cayman

K-5

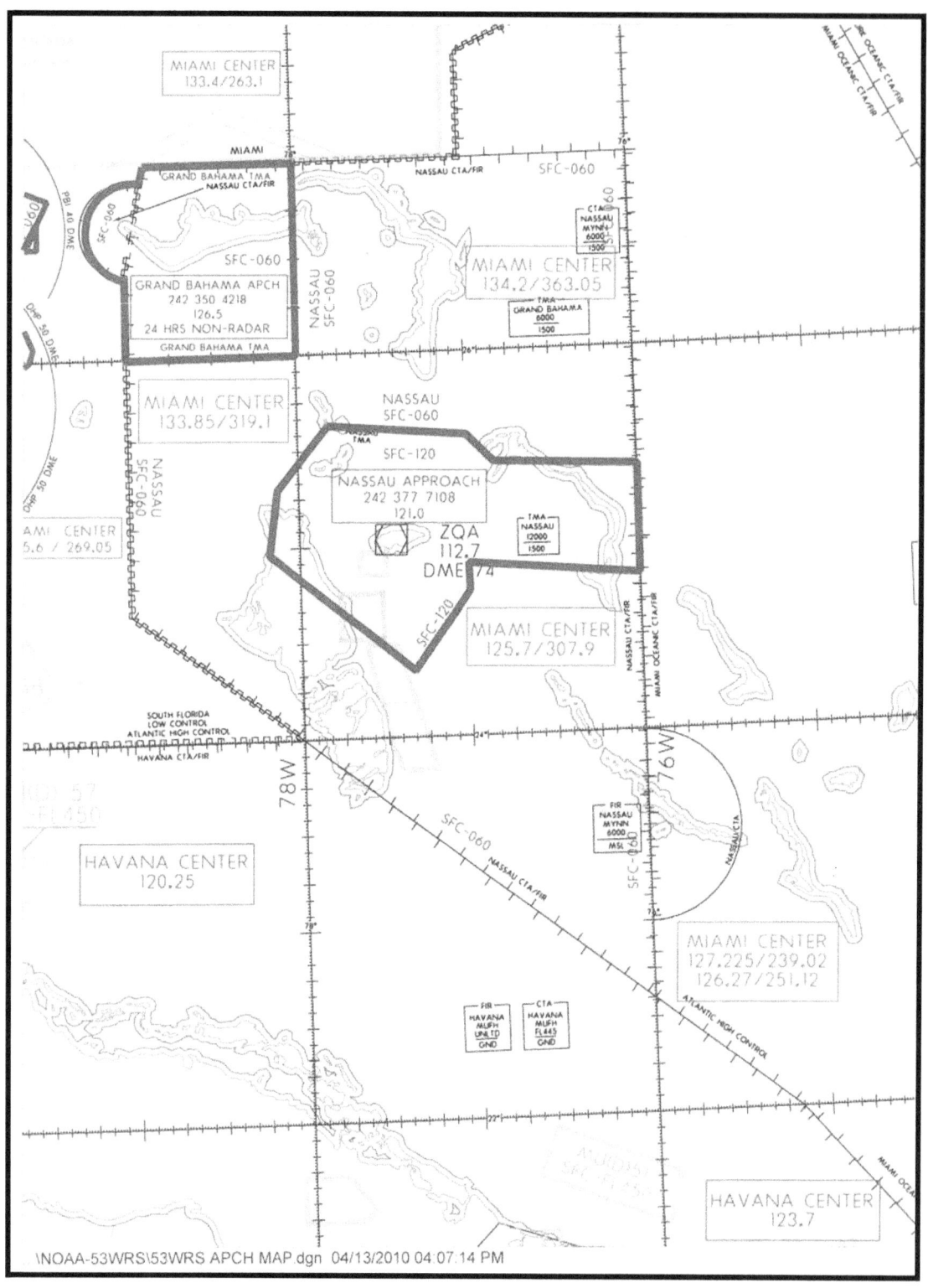

Figure K-6. The Bahamas: Nassau - Freeport

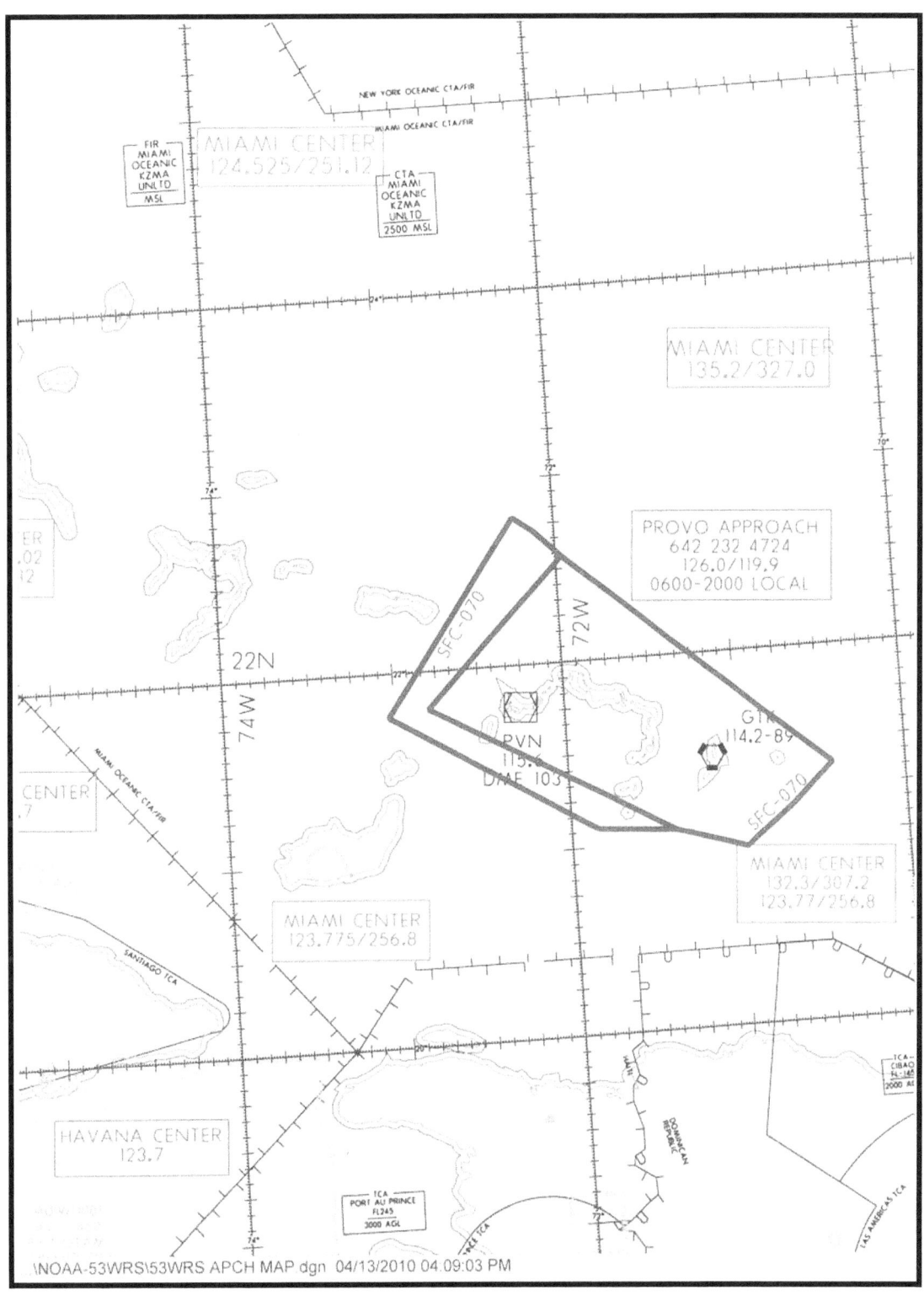

Figure K-7. Turks & Caicos Islands: Grand Turk - Providenciales

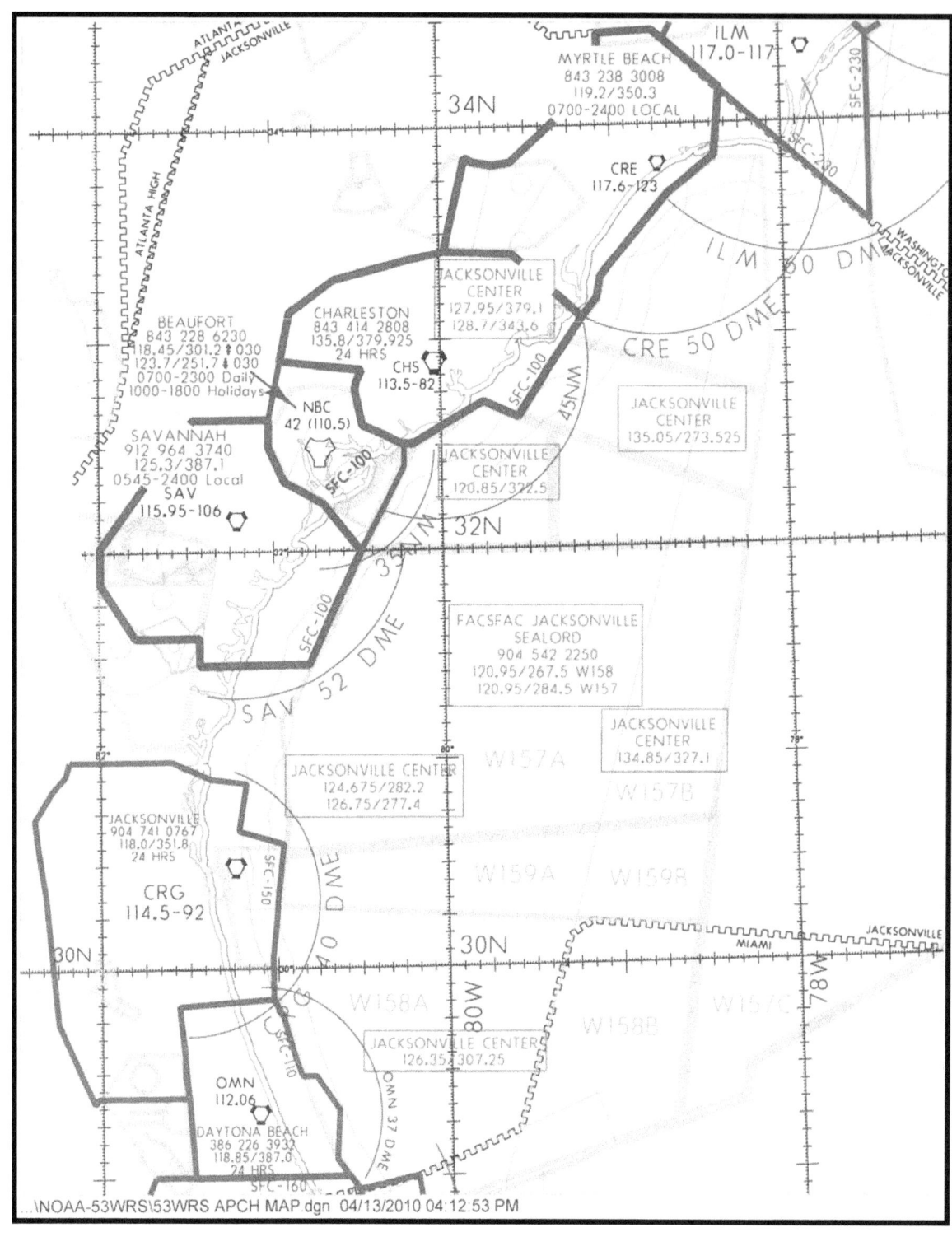

Figure K-8. Daytona Beach, FL – Myrtle Beach, SC

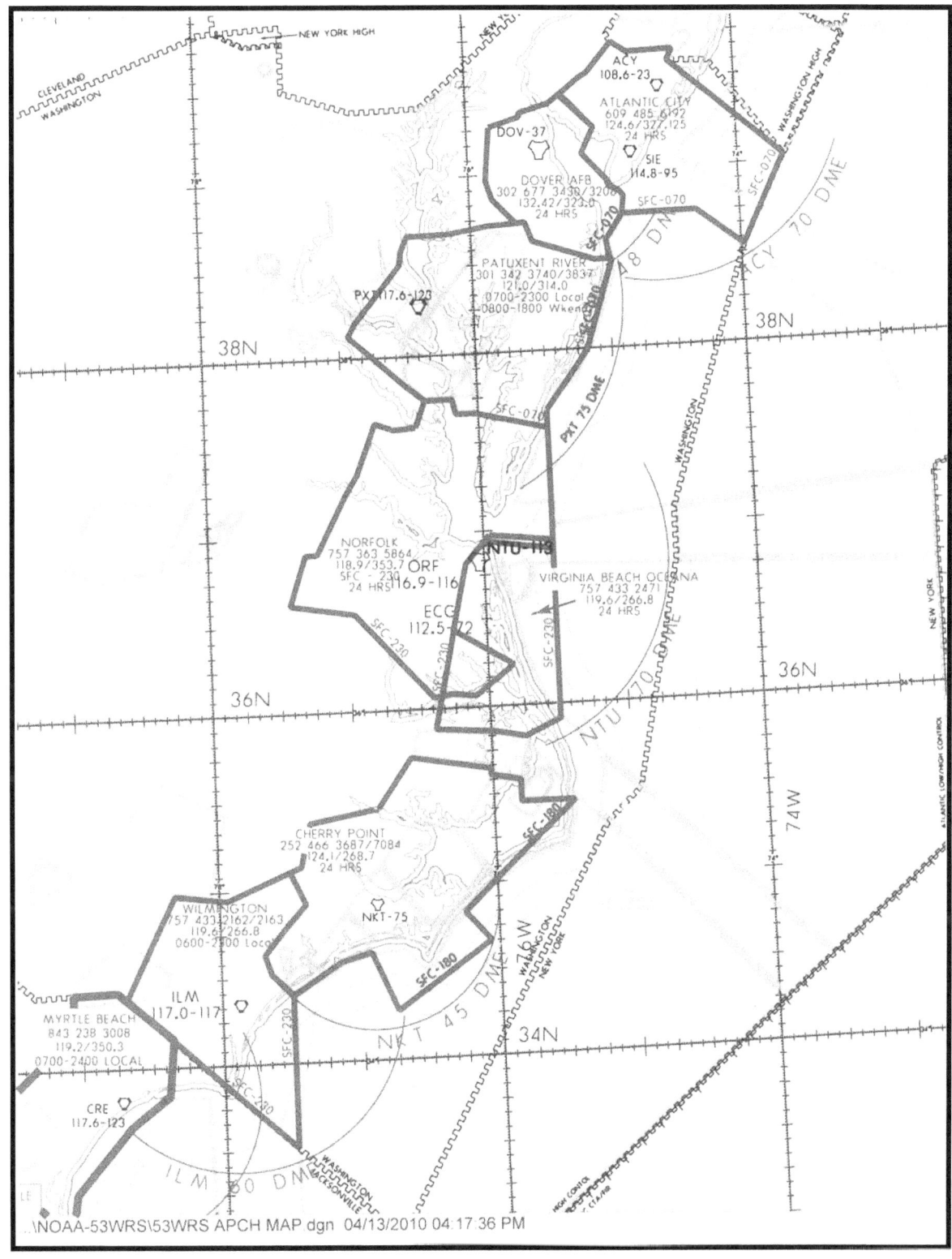

Figure K-9. Wilmington, DE – Atlantic City, NJ

APPENDIX L

MISSION COORDINATION SHEET

1. **Aircraft Call Sign:** _____

2. **TCPOD Number:** _____

3. **Departure & Planned Recovery Airfields:** _____

4. **Route of Flight:** _____

   _____

5. **Storm Center Coordinates:** _____

6. **Radius of Operation from Center Coordinates:** _____

Note: This area excludes the terminal areas (Class D Airspace) and any other airspace within 50 NM of the CONUS shoreline until radio contact is established with ATC.

7. **Expected Entry & Exit Times for Operating Area:**_____

8. **Requested Operating Area Altitude/Block:** _____

9. **Aircraft SATCOM #:** _____

10. **HF SELCAL (if applicable):** _____

11. **NORAD Transponder Code:** _____

12. **POC Contact Information:** _____

APPENDIX M

ACRONYMS/ABBREVIATIONS

-A-

AB	Data type header for Tropical Weather Outlook
AFB	Air Force Base
AFRC	Air Force Reserve Command
AFSATCOM	Air Force Satellite Communications System
AFWA	Air Force Weather Agency
AGL	Above Ground Level
AMSU	Advanced Microwave Sounding Unit
AOC	Aircraft Operations Center (NOAA)
APT	Automatic Picture Transmission
ARGOS	Argos, Inc., a French data collection system
ARINC	Aeronautical Radio, Incorporated
ARSA	Airport Radar Service Area
ARTCC	Air Route Traffic Control Center
ARWO	Aerial Reconnaissance Weather Officer
ASDL	Aircraft-to-Satellite Data Link
ATC	Air Traffic Control
ATCSCC	Air Traffic Control System Command Center
ATSC	Air Traffic Services Cell (DoD; Hq USAF/A3OP)
AVAPS	Advanced Vertical Atmospheric Profiling System
AVHRR	Advanced Very High Resolution Radiometer
AWIPS	Advanced Weather Interactive Processing System

-C-

CARCAH	Chief, Aerial Reconnaissance Coordination, All Hurricanes
CARF	Central Altitude Reservation Function
CERAP	Combined Center RAPCON (FAA)
CFW	Coastal/Lakeshore Hazard Message products (AWIPS Product Category CFW)
C.I.	Current Intensity
C-MAN	Coastal-Marine Automated Network
CNMI	Commonwealth of the Northern Mariana Islands
COM	Commercial (telephone)
CONUS	Continental United States
CPHC	Central Pacific Hurricane Center

-D-

DA	Daylight Ascending
deg	degree (latitude or longitude)
DMSP	Defense Meteorological Satellite Program
DOC	Department of Commerce
DOD	Department of Defense
DOT	Department of Transportation
DPTD	departed
DROP	dropsonde/dropwindsonde
DSN	Defense Switched Network (formerly AUTOVON)

-E-

ESA	European Space Agency
ESPC	Environmental Satellite Processing Center
ETA	Estimated Time of Arrival

-F-

FAA	Federal Aviation Administration
FACSFAC	Fleet Aerial Control and Surveillance Facility
FCMSSR	Federal Committee for Meteorological Services and Supporting Research
FCST	forecast
FCSTR	forecaster
FEA	Flow Evaluation Area (FAA)
FL	flight level
FLT LVL	flight level
FMH	Federal Meteorological Handbook
FNMOC	Fleet Numerical Meteorology and Oceanography Center (USN)
FSM	Federated States of Micronesia
ft	foot/feet

-G-

GAC	Global Area Coverage
GOES	Geostationary Operational Environmental Satellite
GMDSS	Global Maritime Distress and Safety System

-H-

HA	High Accuracy
HD	High Density
HDOB	High Density Observation
HF	High Frequency
hPa	hectopascal/hectopascals
h	hour/hours
HLS	Hurricane Local Statement
HNL	Honolulu (CPHC)
HRD	Hurricane Research Division (NOAA/OAR/AOML)
HRPT	High Resolution Picture Transmission

-I-

ICAO	International Civil Aviation Organization
ICMSSR	Interdepartmental Committee for Meteorological Services and Supporting Research
ID	identification
IFR	Instrument Flight Rules
IOM	International Operations Manager (FAA)
IR	Infrared

-J-

JTWC	Joint Typhoon Warning Center

-K-

km	kilometer/kilometers
KBIX	ICAO identifier for Keesler AFB, MS
KNHC	ICAO identifier for the National Hurricane Center, Miami, FL
kt	knot/knots

-L-

LAC	Local Area Coverage
LI	Long Island

m	meter/meters
MAX	maximum
METEOSAT	European Space Agency geostationary meteorological satellite
MIA	Minimum IFR Altitude
min/MIN	minute
MHS	Microwave Humidity Sounder
mph	mile/miles per hour
MSL	Mean Sea Level
MTSAT-1R	Japanese Geostationary Satellite
MVMT	movement

NASA	National Aeronautics and Space Administration
NAVLANTMETOCFAC	Naval Atlantic Meteorology and Oceanography Facility
NAVMETOCCOM	Naval Meteorology and Oceanography Command
NAVOCEANO	Naval Oceanographic Office
NAVPACMETOCCEN	Naval Pacific Meteorology and Oceanography Center
NAVTRAMETOCFAC	Naval Training Meteorology and Oceanography Facility
NCEP	National Centers for Environmental Prediction (NOAA/NWS)
NCO	NCEP Central Operations
NDBC	National Data Buoy Center
NESDIS	National Environmental Satellite, Data, and Information Service
NHC	National Hurricane Center
NHOP	National Hurricane Operations Plan
nm	nautical miles
NOAA	National Oceanic and Atmospheric Administration
NOM	National Operations Manager (FAA)
NOTAM	Notice to Airmen
NRL	Naval Research Laboratory
NSC	NOAA Science Center
NWS	National Weather Service
NWSOP	National Winter Storms Operations Plan

OAC	Oceanic Aircraft Coordinator (USN)
OB	observation
OFCM	Office of the Federal Coordinator for Meteorological Services and Supporting Research
OM	Operations Manager (FAA)
OMIC	Operations Manager In Charge (FAA)

OPC	Ocean Prediction Center (NCEP)
OSS	Operations Support Squadron (USAF)

-P-

PA	Public Affairs
PHFO	ICAO identifier for Honolulu, HI
POD	Plan of the Day
POES	Polar-Orbiting Environmental Satellite

-R-

RAPCON	Radar Approach Control
RECCO	Reconnaissance Code
RECON	reconnaissance
ROC	Radar Operations Center
RSMC	Regional/Specialized Meteorological Center (WMO)

-S-

SAA	Special Activity Airspace
SAB	Satellite Analysis Branch
SATCOM	Satellite Communications
SFC	surface
SIM	Satellite Interpretation Message
SLP	Sea Level Pressure
SPC	Storm Prediction Center (NCEP)
SSM/I	Special Sensor Microwave Imager (DMSP)
SSM/IS	Special Sensor Microwave Imager Sounder
SSM/T	Special Sensor Microwave Temperature Sounder
STMC	Supervisory Traffic Management Coordinator (FAA)
SUA	Special Use Airspace

-T-

TAFB	Tropical Analysis Forecast Branch (NHC)
TCA	Aviation Tropical Cyclone Advisory
TCD	Tropical Cyclone Discussion
TCM	Tropical Cyclone Forecast/Advisories
TCP	Tropical Cyclone Public Advisory
TCPOD	Tropical Cyclone Plan of the Day
TCR	Tropical Cyclone Reports

TCS	Tropical Cyclone Summary
TCU	Tropical Cyclone Update
TCV	Tropical Cyclone Watch Warning Product
TD	Tropical Depression
TEMP	temperature
TEMP	temporary
TEMP DROP	Dropwindsonde Code
TF	Thermal Fine
TKO	takeoff
TMC	Traffic Management Coordinator (FAA)
T-	Dvorak number Tropical classification number
TRMM	Tropical Rainfall Measurement Mission
TWD	Tropical Weather Discussion
TWO	Tropical Weather Outlook
TWS	Tropical Weather Summary

-U-

UAS	Unmanned Aerial Systems
UAV	Unmanned Aerial Vehicle
UCP	unit control position (WSR-88D)
UHF	Ultra High Frequency
US/U.S.	United States
USAF	United States Air Force
USCG	United States Coast Guard
USN	United States Navy
UTC	Universal Coordinated Time

-V-

VAS	VISSR Atmospheric Sounder
VCP	volume coverage pattern (WSR-88D)
VDM	Vortex Data Message
VIS	Visible
VIIRS	Visible Infrared Imaging Radiometer

-W-

WEFAX	Weather Facsimile
WFO	Weather Forecast Office
WMO	World Meteorological Organization
WND	wind
WPC	Weather Prediction Center (NCEP)

WPMDS	Weather Product Management and Distribution System (Offutt AFB)
WRS	Weather Reconnaissance Squadron
WS	Weather Squadron
WSR-88D	Weather Surveillance Radar-1988 Doppler
WT	Data type header for hurricane bulletins

-Z-

Z	Zulu (UTC)

APPENDIX N

GLOSSARY

-A-

Agency. Any Federal agency or organization participating in the tropical cyclone forecasting and warning service.

Airport Radar Service Area (ARSA). Regulatory airspace surrounding designated airports wherein ATC provides radar vectoring and sequencing on a full-time basis for all IFR and VFR aircraft. The service provided in an ARSA is called ARSA Service which includes: IFR/IFR-standard IFR separation; IFR/VFR-traffic advisories and conflict resolution; and VFR/VFR-traffic advisories and, as appropriate, safety alert. The Airman's Information Manual (AIM) contains an explanation of ARSA. The ARSA's are depicted on VFR aeronautical charts.

Air Traffic Control System Command Center (ATCSCC). The FAA facility that monitors and manages the flow of air traffic throughout the National Airspace System (NAS), producing a safe, orderly, and expeditious flow of traffic while minimizing delays. The ATCSCC is a 24 hour a day, 7 day a week operation.

Air Traffic Services Cell (ATSC). The Air Traffic Services Cell (DoD ATSC/ HAF/A3OP) is a Joint Military and Civil organization which provides liaison, facilitation, and coordination between emergency preparedness and operations organizations as the DoD representative. Additionally the ATSC ensures efficient flow of DoD aircraft in response to wartime mobilization, contingencies, and natural disasters throughout the National Airspace System (NAS). The ATSC is physically located at the FAA ATC Systems Command Center, Warrenton, VA.

-C-

Center Fix. The location of the center of a tropical or subtropical cyclone obtained by means other than reconnaissance aircraft penetration. See also Vortex Fix.

Controlled Airspace. An airspace of defined dimensions within which air traffic control service is provided to IFR flights and to VFR flights in accordance with the airspace classification.

- Controlled airspace is a generic term that covers Class A, Class B, Class C, Class D, and Class E airspace.
- Controlled airspace is also that airspace within which all aircraft operators are subject to certain pilot qualifications, operating rules, and equipment requirements in 14 CFR Part 91 (for specific operating requirements, please refer to 14 CFR Part 91). For IFR operations in any class of controlled airspace, a pilot must file an IFR flight plan and receive an appropriate ATC clearance. Each Class B, Class C, and Class D airspace area designated for an airport contains at least one primary airport around which the airspace is designated (for specific designations and descriptions of the airspace classes, please refer to 14 CFR Part 71).

- Controlled airspace in the United States is designated as follows:

CLASS A: Generally, that airspace from 18,000 feet MSL up to and including FL 600, including the airspace overlying the waters within 12 nautical miles of the coast of the 48 contiguous States and Alaska. Unless otherwise authorized, all persons must operate their aircraft under IFR.

CLASS B: Generally, that airspace from the surface to 10,000 feet MSL surrounding the nations's busiest airports in terms of airport operations or passenger enplanements. The configuration of each Class B airspace area is individually tailored and consists of a surface area and two or more layers (some Class B airspaces areas resemble upside-down wedding cakes), and is designed to contain all published instrument procedures once an aircraft enters the airspace. An ATC clearance is required for all aircraft to operate in the area, and all aircraft that are so cleared receive separation services within the airspace. The cloud clearance requirement for VFR operations is "clear of clouds."

CLASS C: Generally, that airspace from the surface to 4,000 feet above the airport elevation (charted in MSL) surrounding those airports that have an operational control tower, are serviced by a radar approach control, and that have a certain number of IFR operations or passenger enplanements. Although the configuration of each Class C area is individually tailored, the airspace usually consists of a surface area with a 5 nautical mile (NM) radius, a circle with a 10 NM radius that extends no lower than 1,200 feet up to 4,000 feet above the airport elevation and an outer area. Each person must establish two-way radio communications with the ATC facility providing air traffic services prior to entering the airspace and thereafter maintain those communications while within the airspace. VFR aircraft are only separated from IFR aircraft within the airspace.

CLASS D: Generally, that airspace from the surface to 2,500 feet above the airport elevation (charted in MSL) surrounding those airports that have an operational control tower. The configuration of each Class D airspace area is individually tailored and when instrument procedures are published, the airspace will normally be designed to contain the procedures. Arrival extensions for instrument approach procedures may be Class D or Class E airspace. Unless otherwise authorized, each person must establish two-way radio communications with the ATC facility providing air traffic services prior to entering the airspace and thereafter maintain those communications while in the airspace. No separation services are provided to VFR aircraft.

CLASS E: Generally, if the airspace is not Class A, Class B, Class C, or Class D, and it is controlled airspace, it is Class E airspace. Class E airspace extends upward from either the surface or a designated altitude to the overlying or adjacent controlled airspace. When designated as a surface area, the airspace will be configured to contain all instrument procedures. Also in this class are Federal airways, airspace beginning at either 700 or 1,200 AGL used to transition to/from the terminal or en route environment, en route domestic, and offshore airspace areas designated below 18,000 feet MSL. Unless designated at a lower altitude, Class E airspace begins at 14,500 MSL over the United States, including that airspace overlying the waters within 12 nautical miles of the 48 contiguous States and Alaska, up to, but not including 18,000 MSL, and the airspace above FL 600.

Cyclone. An atmospheric closed circulation rotating counter-clockwise in the Northern Hemisphere.

-E-

Extratropical cyclone. A cyclone (of any intensity) for which the primary energy source is baroclinic (i.e., results from the temperature contrast between warm and cold air masses).

Eye. The relatively calm center of the tropical cyclone that is more than one half surrounded by wall cloud.

Eye Wall. An organized band of cumuliform clouds immediately surrounding the center of a tropical cyclone. Eye wall and wall cloud are used synonymously.

-H-

High-Density/High-Accuracy (HD/HA) Data. Those data provided by automated airborne systems--WP-3s or WC-130s equipped with the Improved Weather Reconnaissance System.

Hurricane/Typhoon. A warm-core tropical cyclone in which the maximum sustained surface wind speed (l-min mean) is 64 kt (74 mph) or more.

Hurricane/Typhoon/Tropical Cyclone Season. The portion of the year having a relatively high incidence of hurricanes/typhoons/tropical cyclones. The seasons for the specific areas are as follows (Note: tropical cyclones can occur during any month of the year in the Western Pacific.):

- Atlantic, Caribbean, and the Gulf of Mexico   June 1 to November 30
- Eastern Pacific   May 15 to November 30
- Central Pacific   June 1 to November 30
- Western Pacific   July 1 to December 31

Hurricane Warning Offices. The designated hurricane warning offices follow:

- National Hurricane Center, Miami, Florida
- Central Pacific Hurricane Center, Honolulu, Hawaii

Hurricane/Typhoon Warning. An announcement that sustained winds of 64 knots (74 mph or 119 km/hr) or higher are *expected* somewhere within the specified area in association with a tropical, subtropical, or post-tropical cyclone. Because hurricane preparedness activities become difficult once winds reach tropical storm force, the warning is issued 36 hours in advance of the anticipated onset of tropical-storm-force winds (24 hours for the Western North Pacific). The warning can remain in effect when dangerously high water or a combination of dangerously high water and waves continue, even though winds may be less than hurricane force.

Hurricane/Typhoon Watch. An announcement that sustained winds of 64 knots (74 mph or 119 km/hr) or higher are *possible* within the specified area in association with a tropical, subtropical, or post-tropical cyclone. Because hurricane preparedness activities become difficult once winds reach tropical storm force, the hurricane watch is issued 48 hours in advance of the anticipated onset of tropical storm force winds.

-I-

ICAO-Controlled Airspace. An airspace of defined dimensions within which air traffic control service is provided to IFR flights and to VFR flights in accordance with the airspace classification. (Note: Controlled airspace is a generic term which covers Air Traffic Service airspace Classes A, B, C, D, and E).

-M-

Major Hurricane. A "major" hurricane is one that is classified as a Category 3 or higher.

Maximum 1-Min Sustained Surface Wind. When applied to a particular weather system, refers to the highest 1-minute average wind (at an elevation on 10 meters with an unobstructed exposure) associated with that weather system at a particular point in time.

Micronesia. An area defined by the Commonwealth of the Northern Marianas Islands, the Republic of Palau, the Federated States of Micronesia, and the Republic of the Marshall Islands.

Miles. The term "miles" used in this plan refers to nautical miles (nm) unless otherwise indicated.

Mission Identifier. The nomenclature assigned to tropical and subtropical cyclone aircraft reconnaissance missions for weather data identification. It's an agency-aircraft indicator followed by a Chief, Aerial Reconnaissance Coordination, All Hurricanes (CARCAH) assigned mission-system indicator.

-N-

National Operations Manager. Supervisor in charge of operations of the Air Traffic Control System Command Center.

National Traffic Management Specialist. ATCSCC personnel responsible for the active management of traffic throughout the NAS.

-O-

Operations Manager. Supervisor in charge of operations of an FAA Terminal Radar Approach Control (TRACON).

Operations Manager in Charge. Supervisor in charge of operations of an FAA Air Route Traffic Control Center (ARTCC).

-P-

Post-Tropical Cyclone. A former tropical cyclone. This generic term describes a cyclone that no longer possesses sufficient tropical characteristics to be considered a tropical cyclone. Post-tropical cyclones can continue carrying heavy rains and high winds. Note that former tropical cyclones that have become fully extratropical, as well as remnant lows, are two specific classes of post-tropical cyclones.

Present Movement. The best estimate of the movement of the center of a tropical cyclone at a given time and at a given position. This estimate does not reflect the short-period, small-scale oscillations of the cyclone center.

-R-

Reconnaissance Aircraft Sortie. A flight that meets the requirements of the tropical cyclone plan of the day.

Relocated. A term used in an advisory to indicate that a vector drawn from the preceding advisory position to the latest known position is not necessarily a reasonable representation of the cyclone's movement.

Remnant Low: A post-tropical cyclone that no longer possesses the convective organization required of a tropical cyclone and has maximum sustained winds of less than 34 kt. The term is most commonly applied to the nearly deep-convection-free swirls of stratocumulus in the eastern North Pacific.

-S-

Special Activity Airspace. Any airspace with defined dimensions within the National Airspace System wherein limitations may be imposed upon aircraft operations. This airspace may be restricted areas, prohibited areas, military operations areas, air ATC assigned airspace, and any other designated airspace areas. The dimensions of this airspace are programmed into URET and can be designated as either active or inactive by screen entry. Aircraft trajectories are constantly tested against the applicable sectors when violations are predicted.

Special Use Airspace. Airspace of defined dimensions identified by an area on the surface of the earth wherein activities must be confined because of their nature and/or wherein limitations may be imposed upon aircraft operations that are not a part of those activities. Types of special use airspace are:

a   Alert Area- Airspace which may contain a high volume of pilot training activities or an unusual type of aerial activity, neither of which is hazardous to aircraft. Alert Areas are depicted on aeronautical charts for the information of nonparticipating pilots. All activities within an Alert Area are conducted in accordance with Federal Aviation Regulations, and pilots of participating aircraft as well as pilots transiting the area are equally responsible for collision avoidance.

b   Controlled Firing Area- Airspace wherein activities are conducted under conditions so controlled as to eliminate hazards to nonparticipating aircraft and to ensure the safety of persons and property on the ground.

c   Military Operations Area (MOA)- A MOA is airspace established outside of Class A airspace area to separate or segregate certain nonhazardous military activities from IFR traffic and to identify for VFR traffic where these activities are conducted.

   (Refer to AIM.)

d   Prohibited Area- Airspace designated under 14 CFR Part 73 within which no person may operate an aircraft without the permission of the using agency.

   (Refer to AIM.)
   (Refer to En Route Charts.)

e   Restricted Area- Airspace designated under 14 CFR Part 73, within which the flight of aircraft, while not wholly prohibited, is subject to restriction. Most restricted areas are designated joint use and IFR/VFR operations in the area may be authorized by the controlling ATC facility when it is not being utilized by the using agency. Restricted areas are depicted on en route charts. Where joint use is authorized, the name of the ATC controlling facility is also shown.

   (Refer to 14 CFR Part 73.)
   (Refer to AIM.)

f   Warning Area- A warning area is airspace of defined dimensions extending from 3 nautical miles outward from the coast of the United States, that contains activity that may be hazardous to nonparticipating aircraft. The purpose of such warning area is to warn nonparticipating pilots of the potential danger. A warning area may be located over domestic or international waters or both.

Storm Surge. An abnormal rise in sea level accompanying a hurricane or other intense storm, and whose height is the difference between the observed level of the sea surface and the level that would have occurred in the absence of the cyclone. Storm surge is usually estimated by subtracting the normal or astronomic tide from the observed storm tide.

Storm Tide. The actual level of sea water resulting from the astronomic tide combined with the storm surge.

Subtropical Cyclone. A non-frontal low-pressure system that has characteristics of both tropical and extratropical cyclones. Like tropical cyclones, they are non-frontal, synoptic-scale cyclones that originate over tropical or subtropical waters, and have a closed surface wind circulation about a well-defined center. In addition, they have organized moderate to deep convection, but lack a central dense overcast. Unlike tropical cyclones, subtropical cyclones derive a significant proportion of their energy from baroclinic sources, and are generally cold-core in the upper troposphere, often being associated with an upper-level low or trough. In comparison to tropical cyclones, these systems generally have a radius of maximum winds occurring relatively far from the center (usually greater than 60 nm), and generally have a less symmetric wind field and distribution of convection.

Subtropical Depression. A subtropical cyclone in which the maximum sustained surface wind speed (l-min mean) is 33 knots (38 mph) or less.

Subtropical Storm. A subtropical cyclone in which the maximum sustained surface wind speed (1-min mean) is 34 knots (39 mph) or higher.

Super Typhoon. A "super" typhoon is one that is classified as having winds of 130 knots (150 mph) or greater.

Sustained Surface Wind. The 1-minute averaged wind at the 10-meter elevation with an unobstructed exposure.

Synoptic Surveillance (formerly Synoptic Track).Weather reconnaissance mission flown to provide vital meteorological information in data sparse ocean areas as a supplement to existing surface, radar, and satellite data. Synoptic flights better define the upper atmosphere and aid in the prediction of tropical cyclone motion and intensity.

-T-

Tropical Cyclone. A warm-core, non-frontal synoptic-scale cyclone, originating over tropical or subtropical waters, with organized deep convection and a closed surface wind circulation about a well-defined center.

Tropical Cyclone Plan of the Day. A coordinated mission plan that tasks operational weather reconnaissance requirements during the next 1100 to 1100Z UTC day or as required, describes reconnaissance flights committed to satisfy both operational and research requirements, and identifies possible reconnaissance requirements for the succeeding 24-hour period.

Tropical Depression. A tropical cyclone in which the maximum sustained surface wind speed (l-min mean) is 33 kt (38 mph) or less.

Tropical Disturbance. A discrete tropical weather system of apparently organized convection-- generally 100 to 300 mi in diameter--originating in the tropics or subtropics, having a nonfrontal migratory character, and maintaining its identity for 24 hours or more. It may or may not be associated with a detectable perturbation of the wind field.

Tropical Storm. A tropical cyclone in which the maximum sustained surface wind speed (l-min mean) ranges from 34 kt (39 mph) to 63 kt (73 mph).

Tropical Storm Warning. An announcement that sustained winds of 34 to 63 knots (39 to73 mph or 63 to 118 km/hr) are *expected* within 36 hours within the specified coastal area in association with a tropical, subtropical or post-tropical cyclone. NHC, CPHC, and WFO Guam issue warnings when conditions are *expected* within 36 hours.

Tropical Storm Watch. An announcement that sustained winds of 34 to 63 knots (39 to 73 mph or 63 to 118 km/hr) are *possible* somewhere in the specified area within 48 hours in association with a tropical, subtropical or post-tropical cyclone. NHC, CPHC, and WFO Guam issue watches when conditions are *possible* within 48 hours.

Tropical Wave. A trough or cyclonic curvature maximum in the trade-wind easterlies. The wave may reach maximum amplitude in the lower middle troposphere or may be the reflection of an upper tropospheric cold low or equatorial extension of a middle latitude trough.

Tropical Weather System. A designation for one of a series of tropical weather anomalies. As such, it is the basic generic designation, which in successive stages of intensification, may be classified as a tropical disturbance, wave, depression, storm, or hurricane.

Typhoon/Hurricane. A warm-core tropical cyclone in which the maximum sustained surface wind speed (l-min mean) is 64 kt (74 mph) or more.

-U-

Uncontrolled Airspace (Class G Airspace). That portion of the airspace that has not been designated as Class A, Class B, Class C, Class D, or Class E and within which Air Traffic Control has neither the authority nor the responsibility for exercising control over air traffic.

-V-

Vortex Fix. The location of the surface and/or flight level center of a tropical or subtropical cyclone obtained by reconnaissance aircraft penetration. See Center Fix, also.

Wall Cloud. An organized band of cumuliform clouds immediately surrounding the center of a tropical cyclone. Wall cloud and eye wall are used synonymously.

www.ingramcontent.com/pod-product-compliance
Lightning Source LLC
Chambersburg PA
CBHW081212280526
45787CB00006B/2394